# THE AUTHORS

Dr. David Farmer is the official historian of Swansea City A.F.C. and a director of the club which he has followed since 1938. He is the author of many books, including *Swansea Town/City 1912-1982*; *Giants of Post War Welsh Rugby*; and *The All Whites*. In addition, he has been a contributor to the Swans' match programme for more than twenty years. A native of Swansea, he was educated at Dynevor School and the Universities of Manchester and Bath. He is Emeritus Professor at Henley, Visiting Professor at Birmingham and Bath Universities and Deputy Chairman of the Tŷ Olwen Trust.

Peter Stead, born in Barry in 1943, was, until his retirement, Senior Lecturer in History at the University of Wales, Swansea. He has also twice been a Fulbright Scholar in the United States, at Wellesley College, Massachusetts, and at the University of North Carolina. He is the author of several books, including *Film and the Working Class*; *The Feature Film in British and American Society* (1989) and the biographical studies *Richard Burton* (1991) and *Dennis Potter* (1993). He is the co-author of *Heart and Soul: The Character of Welsh Rugby* (1998).

Peter Stead is a frequent broadcaster and presenter, panellist and commentator on political and cultural issues. He has been an Executive Member of the Welsh Academy and a Labour Parliamentary Candidate. He is a Committee Member of the Welsh Sports Hall of Fame and has been a lifelong supporter of Cardiff City and the Swans.

# IVOR ALLCHURCH
## M.B.E.

*The Authorised Biography
of the
Legendary Golden Boy*

David Farmer
&
Peter Stead

CHRISTOPHER DAVIES PUBLISHERS
*in conjunction with*

**South Wales Evening Post**

Copyright © 1998 David Farmer and Peter Stead

First Impression: November 1998
Reprinted: December 1998

Published in 1998 by
Christopher Davies (Publishers) Ltd.
P.O. Box 403, Swansea, SA1 4YF.

The right of David Farmer and Peter Stead to be
identified as the Authors of the Work has been
asserted by them in accordance with the Copyright,
Designs and Patents Act 1988.

A CIP catalogue record for this book is
available from the British Library.

ISBN 0 7154 0733 3

Printed and bound in Wales by
Dinefwr Press Ltd.
Rawlings Road, Llandybie
Carmarthenshire, SA18 3YD.

# Contents

# Illustration Acknowledgements

The following list shows the origin of each illustration which is included in this book. Reasonable care has been taken to ensure that proper reference has been made in each case. Where it has not been possible to identify the originator of the photograph or drawing, the person who loaned the item to the authors is cited. The authors wish to thank all concerned for their assistance in helping to ensure that the book is well illustrated.

*Trevor and Ivor in tandem.*

# Foreword

I had left Swansea Town before Ivor Allchurch came on the scene there, but my family kept me in touch with what was going on at the Vetch Field. As far as I can remember, the first time I heard the name Allchurch was from my father who had seen a young blond boy playing for the Swans reserves. Joe Sykes, who looked after the youngsters at the Vetch, told my dad that the boy was going to be one of the greats. After seeing him play, my dad agreed, and he and Joe were proved to be absolutely right. In my opinion, Ivor Allchurch was one of the greatest British footballers of all time.

When I was playing for Aston Villa and Wales I was kept in touch with the development of 'Young Allchurch' by the players from Swansea Town who were in the Welsh team with me. These were people like Billy Lucas and Roy Paul, both outstanding players in their own right. Each of them was convinced that Ivor was exceptional, and Billy told me that the youngster would be in the Welsh team before long. And once the lad made his début (at the same time as another Swansea boy, Ray Daniel) they didn't even think about replacing him.

From my point of view as a centre forward, Ivor was a gem. He could thread short passes through the eye of a needle, or make sweeping thirty, or forty-yarders to open up defences. Even when gaining his first 'caps' he was prepared to take-on experienced internationals, and it looked to me as if he worried them far more than they worried him. From the beginning he had outstanding ball control, a wicked body swerve, and he could hit a dead ball like a mule. Also he wasn't worried by the vicious tackles of some wing halves who opposed him and who set out to stop him by less than fair means.

I remember one match when a Scotsman – who shall be nameless here – hacked him to the ground three times in quick succession. And, in those days, the heavy boots which we wore could cause real damage. But, each time, Ivor got up, rubbed his leg and limped away to get on with the game. He didn't even protest to the referee. At half time I said to him, 'Why don't you kick him back, Ivor?' 'Don't worry, Trev,' he replied, 'I'll go past him next time.' And he did, leaving the player on all fours in the middle of the field. As the boxers say, after that he didn't lay a glove on Ivor.

Everyone who played with Ivor Allchurch (and many who played against him) will tell you the same thing about him. He was a gentleman on and off the pitch. I remember one game when he scored a goal from a miss-hit shot. Before he ran back to the centre, he apologised to a couple of the other team's defenders. 'Sorry boys, that was lucky. I didn't hit it properly.' Most people wouldn't have said a word.

Because we were both Swansea boys with similar backgrounds (he was born about a half mile from where I used to live), we had a lot in common. I enjoyed his company on many occasions. We roomed together for a couple of international trips and, just as he was in the dressing room, he was as quiet as a mouse. He was shy and, quite frankly, I don't believe that he ever realised how good he really was. But, then, that was true of many tremendous young footballers who emerged from the Swansea schools around that time. People like Jack Kelsey, Ray Daniel, Cliff Jones, Terry Medwin and John Charles. The 'Busby Babes' were a marvellous group of players, but in my opinion, these boys, all born in Swansea, were at least their equal. And Ivor stood out even among them.

Many people in talking about modern football and the kind of money which current players are paid, have asked me what Ivor would be worth today? I generally say 'Priceless', because that fits him best. But, put it this way, there are very, very few of today's stars who could hold a candle to Ivor Allchurch at his peak. What's more, whoever bought Ivor Allchurch got 200% effort for their money. He must have been a manager's dream!

There *was* only one Ivor Allchurch! He was an outstanding player, with a lovely, generous way with him. Despite all his fame he never forgot himself. It was a privilege to know him and to play with him and I consider myself to be lucky to have done so. That is why I was delighted to be approached to contribute this foreword for Ivor's story. I always felt that there should have been a book written about the man they called 'The Golden Boy'. When he was playing he was an inspiration to thousands of fans and to many, many men who played with him. Perhaps now, this story will inspire all those who read it.

*Trevor Ford*

# Preface

The origins of this book can be traced to the day of Ivor's funeral at Morriston Crematorium, Swansea. The authors, along with countless others, thronged the forecourt as the service proceeded inside the packed chapel. Famous footballers of yesteryear rubbed shoulders with dignitaries, officials, the Press, T.V. and radio, as well as ordinary fans of the player generally recognised to have been one of the greatest footballers of all time. All were there, not only to express their sympathy to Ivor's family, but to pay tribute to the man who was an icon in Wales and on Tyneside; a man who personified all that is good in the game; a footballer who thrilled spectators all over the world; and a man whose demeanour attracted thousands of tributes during his career and long after he had finished playing.

After the service, as the crowd dispersed and hundreds of memories of the man they called 'The Golden Boy' were shared, the authors found themselves proposing, almost simultaneously, that a book should be written about Ivor – for none existed. We felt that, given his stature in the game and the enjoyment which he had given to so many, it was important that his story should be recorded for posterity. We believed it would be a story which would be savoured by all who had seen him play, whilst providing those who will have only heard about 'Ivor' with a record of his life.

We were inspired to write the book by the simple fact that there can never be another Ivor Allchurch. Apart from anything else, given the environment within which modern footballers grow up and live, it would be impossible for any one of them to develop the same attitudes as Ivor John Allchurch. Ivor was a boy and a man of his era; an era which has passed into sociological history along with close-knit mining communities, the predominance of the chapel, and the tanner ball in traffic-free streets. An era when, for the majority, sport provided the major escape from the rigours of the workaday world. Consequently, even in the unlikely event that someone with Allchurch ability should be discovered, his attitudes and his expectations would be significantly different from those of Ivor. In the media dominated soccer arena of the present day, quiet, gentle, unassuming geniuses would appear to be an extinct species.

This book, therefore, is a story which will evoke nostalgia in those who lived through the age in question, and wonder in those who were born later or who are to come. However, all who read the book will find they will obtain a common benefit; they will gain an understanding of a remarkable man! A gentleman in every sense. A sporting genius with an outstanding battery of footballing skills and vision which are found in very, very few.

Having known the man and having seen him play, we have to confess that we started our work on this book in a frame of mind which was hardly objective. We were both unashamed 'Ivor fans'. Yet, given that both of us spent the bulk of our careers as university teachers, it was necessary for us to challenge our preconceptions. But we have to say that our extensive research into the life and times of Ivor Allchurch has served only to reinforce our initial position. Ivor, we found, was all we believed him to be. Indeed he was, if anything, greater than the mythology which has grown around him would suggest. As the reader will perceive, our conclusions are based upon what has been written and said about him by so many people and in so many ways. Sir Tom Finney put it eloquently: 'Ivor Allchurch was a gentleman footballer of the first order, who represented all that is good in the game.' It will be surprising if, after reading this book, the reader does not come to the same conclusion.

*Acknowledgements*

It will be clear from the text which follows that our research has involved discussion and correspondence with many people. We have been helped by so many that it would be impossible, in the space available, to thank each and every one by name. Whilst several who have been of particular assistance are listed below, we wish to place on record our thanks to everyone who has helped us during the last fourteen months. Without that help we could not have produced this book.

Men who played with and against Ivor were, of course, a key source of information. From them we learnt about Ivor the footballer and Ivor the man. Among those who willingly talked with us about our subject were: Len Allchurch, Mel Charles, Sir Bobby Charlton, Alan Durban, Terry Elwell, Sir Tom Finney, Trevor Ford, Alan Harrington, Bobby Henning, Cliff Jones, Tom Kiley, Terry Medwin, Mel Nurse, Ron Stitfall, Bob Stokoe, and Colin Webster.

Ivor's sister Dilys, his boyhood friends, Ivor Williams and Derek Thomas, and his schoolmaster, Mr Hugh Sinnett, all assisted our understanding of the young Ivor, whilst our knowledge of his adult life was increased for us by his wife, Mrs. Esme Allchurch who was so much a part of it from the age of sixteen. Her insights, of course, were particularly valuable in informing us about a very private man, and we are grateful to her for her willing co-operation throughout the researching and writing of this book.

Statistical information about Ivor's career at Newcastle and Cardiff was willingly provided by Paul Joannou and Mark Adams respectively.

A long-time collaborator, Brian Lile unearthed useful information for us from the bowels of the National Library of Wales and assisted us with Welsh language sources, and Sir Glanmor Williams, who saw Ivor play in those halcyon days of the fifties, was, as ever, a great source of inspiration and advice. We are grateful to both of them.

At the *South Wales Evening Post*, who are co-publishers of this book, Editor, George Edwards, Sports Editor, David Evans, John Burgam, Senior Soccer Correspondent, and Barbara Powell, Photographic Archivist, were all of assistance to us. For his part, Christopher Davies our publisher was enthusiastic about the project from the outset and was a willing supporter of our efforts.

At Gwasg Dinefwr Press, our printers, we received outstanding service, as ever, from Donald, Eddie, Emyr and Stephen for which we are grateful.

Antonio Carra of Kristys Bakery, Sketty was kind enough to translate for us many Italian news stories about Ivor, we are grateful to him. Jill Isaac, once again, turned our inexpert typing into quality disks ready for the printer, which was appreciated by them as much as us.

We would like to thank the County Archivist, Susan Beckley and her staff, particularly Gwyn Davies and Norman Armes, for giving us ready access to the appropriate records which are under their care. Thanks, too, to the staff at Swansea's Reference Library who were extremely helpful.

Gordon Daniels, who was Secretary at the Vetch Field, provided helpful insights into 'behind the scenes' happenings at the Vetch, and Peter

Corrigan and Huw Richards, two well-known sporting journalists were also helpful in a variety of ways and we wish to acknowledge that, as we do the work of the numerous journalists whose reports and insights provided so much information for us about Ivor. For the cover design we are indebted to Llewellyn Thomas of Swansea who took immense trouble to convert our rough-spun drawing into an attractive cover. Thanks are due, too, to Richard Shepherd and Mel Nurse for providing interesting photographs which filled gaps which otherwise would have existed.

Finally, we wish to record our sincere appreciation of the trust placed in us by Esme Allchurch and the wider family when we set out to write this book. We hope that our efforts to tell Ivor's story in an honest and objective manner have resulted in a work of which they can be proud.

*David Farmer & Peter Stead*

Swansea
November 1998

# The Golden Boy

With every justification the 1940's and 1950's have been recalled as a 'Golden Age' of British Football. In those days, as austerity gradually gave way to some degree of affluence, millions of British soccer fans drew considerable pleasure from their role within a distinctive football culture. That role involved regular attendance at greatly loved old grounds in town and city centres where huge crowds of up to 70,000 roared, sighed and applauded as one; it involved the careful perusal of football programmes as well as the sports pages of morning and evening papers, being home in time to listen to Radio's *Sports Report* and subscribing to *Charles Buchan's Football Monthly*.

There was a wonderfully gratifying homogeneity about that football culture. Accents might vary enormously; nearly all fans and players spoke with heavy and sometimes incomprehensible accents, loyalties were fierce, judgements admittedly subjective, and yet for all this apparent diversity the committed followers of football had much in common. Their incomes, lifestyle and educational background were all very similar; they had nearly all played football regularly at school or for local clubs; and they were all fantastically knowledgeable about the rules of the game, its techniques, possibilities and personnel. Effortlessly they could reel off the normal team line-ups of every First Division team and for many of the leading clubs in the lower divisions. Not only could they confidently name all the players, they could rate them too. Inevitably their clear favourites would play for the local team, either as home-grown talent or as headline-catching transfers, but they would also have heroes who played for other teams, and nothing gave them greater pleasure than the fanciful selection of a favourite side in which the local tyros could be lined up alongside household names from glamour clubs and which featured, too, generally neglected and underrated geniuses from unfashionable outfits in far-flung corners of the land.

What was also pleasing about this football culture was its genuinely

*Weighing up his 'caps' – Ivor in 1962.*

British dimension. It was a culture that was overwhelmingly dominated by the English Football League but, of course, the clubs in that League, including the four Welsh clubs, drew very heavily on Scottish talent and to a lesser extent on Welsh and Irish talent too. Indeed, it can be argued that true Britishness was more fully evident in the players of the English league system of those years than in anything since Lord Kitchener's army in the First World War. The English fans fully appreciated the Celtic element that added colour and distinction to their leagues, whilst in Ireland, Scotland and Wales there was a constant process of checking to see which favourite sons were transforming the fortunes of various English sides. The League and the FA Cup were the true measure of a player's greatness; but Britishness was also confirmed by the added bonus of the annual Home International Championship which bound England to regular matches with Scotland, Wales and Northern Ireland on a home-and-away basis in alternate seasons. England had many players to choose from, whereas the other nations often had to worry about the quality of their selections in key positions. Nevertheless, a handful of Celtic geniuses backed up by team spirit was often enough to frighten England and occasionally to beat them. Home internationals prompted fans into choosing a British team and what was remarkable in that fun exercise was how often fans found themselves distributing places to the four nations on a fairly even basis. It was indeed a British football culture.

The Home Internationals served as a reminder of the game's origins in Victorian times and in fact there were many other aspects of football's character that revealed how deeply rooted it was in the nation's history. Only those who had some understanding of the story of the Industrial Revolution could fully appreciate the nuances of the game's geographical pattern. It could probably be proved that football fans had a more complete knowledge of the nation's railway system and distribution of towns than other citizens. Non-followers of the game might be surprised that both Liverpool and Nottingham had two teams that played in grounds less than a mile apart, and that some of the best teams in the country played in comparatively small industrial towns in central Lancashire. True fans knew all these facts and could go on to tell you all you wanted to know about Accrington Stanley, Port Vale and Tranmere Rovers. What is more, no real fan would find it odd that a small town like Burnley was the home of a team that was regularly contending for the First Division Championship or that individual players of world ranking played week in and week out for Preston North End, Blackburn Rovers, Blackpool, Hull City and Middlesbrough. They knew that football success was born out of history, enthusiasm and loyalty; money was needed too but the wealthy directors who organised that money were legitimised by the extent to which they operated within and confirmed that troika of values. Out of history, football had forged its own geography and its own distribution of both loyalty and talent. That is why in this 'golden age' no genuine fan would be at all surprised if you boasted that your own humble side contained the best player in the land. What is truly glorious about those years is that more often than not you were believed. This, then, was the football culture that bred Ivor Allchurch. Throughout his career he was to exemplify all its best features.

Across the land people knew of Ivor and for many years his name was largely synonymous with Swansea. 'Where are you from?', one would be asked, or more usually, 'Who do you support?', and the mere mention of 'Swansea' would be enough to elicit the immediate response: 'Ivor Allchurch'. Fans read about him in match programmes although, as had been implied, they hardly needed them as far as team line-ups were concerned. If Swansea Town were named on the cover then sure enough Ivor would be at inside-left wearing No. 10. But, as Sir Matt Busby once commented in a marvellous and entirely appropriate tribute, Ivor 'never needed a number on his back' for his polish and class were unmistakable. In fact almost everything about him was unmistakable. In those days footballers came in a far greater variety of physical shape and size and, indeed, one reason for the game's popularity in urban Britain was the way it catered for all the types to be found in the average terraced row, village or school class. Michael Parkinson once provided a useful guide for readers who could not remember those days when horribly ugly gnarled legs determined full-backs and wing-halves, frailty wingers, madness goalies, robustness centre-forwards, ranginess and thick skulls centre-halves and vision inside-forwards, with the distinct probability that the inside-left would be a consumptive intellectual. That final tag could never have been applied to Ivor but, even if he had appeared without a number, a crowd to whom he was a stranger would have spotted him immediately as the side's thinker, the ideas man, the passer, the genius, the player who would make things happen, and all that would have been obvious even as he ran out for the warm-up. Already he stood out, for there was a studied and yet natural elegance about the man, a refinement that was clinched by his unnaturally blond and wavy hair. Most fans saw him first wearing the white of Swansea, and that too invested him with a slightly unnatural and perhaps even priestly aura: there was, even before the kick-off, a presence and potential about this No. 10 which promised a new dimension – and a challenging one if he was in the opposing team.

In the game itself all that class and polish to which Sir Matt referred soon became evident. There was a rhythm and flow to Ivor's play that will become very familiar as his playing career is recalled. He was usually to be found just inside his opponent's half, either in or adjacent to the centre circle. On receiving the ball he would instinctively turn to shield it from any opponent before looking up and passing the ball immaculately either to a nearby colleague or, more usually to a waiting winger some thirty yards distant. Now this was prettily done and suitably applauded, but it was par for the course and almost every team in the land had a visionary who instinctively passed the ball in such a way as to convince the crowd that he could 'do it with his eyes closed'. But Ivor was more than a slide rule passer. There was his control, his balance, his grace, his ability to dictate the pace of the game and to unlock midfield stalemates, but even more there was the way in which his whole body would suddenly be capable of changing the general rhythm of the game with just a sudden surge of energy that for him seemed utterly natural. That surge might involve a body swerve; that was one of his hallmarks and John Crooks once memorably referred to the way in which Ivor was capable of sending 10,000 people behind the goal 'the wrong way'. There could be quick one-twos with other forwards and then a short sprint followed by a surprisingly powerful and direct shot or a cruelly effective chipped shot, for he was a genuine finisher to a far greater extent that most mere 'passers'. If a goal had been scored he would turn quickly to get on with the game but there was always just a hint of a smile that conveyed real pleasure. If the shot hit the bar or narrowly missed he would simply shrug, gently flicking out his lower arms as the crowd shared his sense not so much of the game's frustrations as of its exhilarating tension. Every game was like this with no dissent, no anger, just a recital of skills within the shape and form of the team game that had its own course to run. Some games were won, others were drawn or lost but always there was the rhythm, the expectation, the moments of sheer delight, the poetry. Watching Ivor play was a confirmation of how life, however humdrum, allowed instances of utterly natural grace and excellence.

The recognition of Ivor's stature was an integral part of Swansea's identity throughout the 1950's. The town was of medium size, already beginning to lose its distinction as a world-renowned metallurgical centre and already, too, losing out to Cardiff which was to be confirmed as capital of Wales in 1955. Furthermore Swansea was a divided town for it was the home of one of the world's most famous club rugby sides, the All Whites, who playing at St Helen's had beaten all

*'The Golden Boy' – a photograph used in a Quaker Oats advertisement.*

the great touring sides including the dreaded New Zealand 'All Blacks'. Nevertheless, for the vast majority of Swansea's 150,000 citizens it was the game of association football which gave the town its distinction; and it was the neat, old-fashioned intimate Vetch Field, located right in the town centre and sheltered from Swansea Bay and Atlantic storms only by a Victorian prison, which was the clearest indication that Swansea was very much part of the British mainstream. The town glorified in its soccer talent, in the way that the school teams of its inner suburbs of tightly packed terraced houses produced young player after young player with remarkable ball skills. Nearly all British teams realised that success came by blending the home grown with talented imports, but in the 1950's there were to be heady moments in Swansea when it seemed as if a successful Second Division side could be fielding a team consisting entirely of young men born and bred within five miles of the Vetch. Of course, not all the local talent could be retained. Of the five world greats that the town sensationally produced in this era the immensely talented John Charles (born in Swansea in 1931) went straight from the Vetch's groundstaff to Leeds before playing any games for the Swans; that handsome and fearless centre-forward Trevor Ford (born in Swansea in 1927) had a couple of seasons only for his home team before going on to Aston Villa; goalkeeper Jack Kelsey (born in Swansea in 1929) was a Swans supporter but was signed by Arsenal directly from his village side, whilst Cliff Jones, the most exciting of wingers (born in Swansea in 1935) , had five years for the Swans before joining Spurs. But Ivor Allchurch (born in Swansea in 1929) stayed far longer and so became the most beloved and admired of the Famous Five. Throughout the 1950's he was the star at the Vetch, he was the town's talisman and the hallmark of its footballing class. The production line went on (there were always local lads to fill up the team) but it was Ivor who was there to prompt them and to bring them on; if they were any good it was Ivor who would prove it.

It was the English League's Second Division which established Ivor's reputation and his place in the affections of Swansea people, but whilst still only twenty-one he had made his début for Wales and so was launched on an international career which lasted sixteen years and which gained him admirers throughout the world. Ivor was soon established as the 'Golden Boy' of Welsh soccer; he was as distinctive and unmistakable in his impressively formal red Welsh shirt as in the white of the Swans, and straight away it was recognised that his skills were absolutely indispensable. More than any other player, including his fellow Swansea-born greats, Ivor became the fixture in the Welsh team. He was almost an ever-present for Wales, and it was very often the case, especially, as it happens, in later years, that it was his presence in the side that guaranteed that Wales would display true international quality. It was always thought entirely appropriate that in his era Ivor should break all the records relating to appearances and goal-scoring for Wales.

It was the international dimension that confirmed Ivor's standing in the world and culture of British football. *Charles Buchan's Football Monthly* and other publications would frequently include him in their best team on the basis of his league performances, but it was his Welsh credentials which allowed him his unchallenged place as one of the greatest British footballers, and which prompted fans to select him for their Best of British teams. Ivor's right to be counted with the best was proved as early as 1951 when in his seventh game for Wales he helped his country celebrate its 75th Anniversary as a footballing nation by scoring twice against the Rest of the United Kingdom at Ninian Park, Cardiff. All international games were taken seriously in those days but there was no doubt that for Wales it was the annual match against England which ranked above all games. In 1955 Ivor played his part as Wales defeated England 2-1 in a match that suggested to all welsh fans that the game had truly come of age in the Principality. Remarkably, one of Ivor's greatest games was to come ten years later when Bobby Moore's England, in the midst of building for a World Cup they were to win, were held to a goalless draw at Cardiff. There were often occasions in the 1950's and 1960's when English managers wished that the Welsh No. 10 was playing for them.

Over the years there were exotic locations and intriguing fixtures as Wales fulfilled its commitments but increasingly the ultimate arbitrator of football standing was becoming the World Cup. For years the British had not taken it very seriously but now air travel and television had made it the focus of world football. If you were good, you did well in the World Cup Finals. Well, Wales *were* good in the World Cup Finals which were played in Sweden in 1958. It is true that they were lucky to be there at all, but in the event they made the most of it. In fact they got to the quarter finals; with just a little more luck they might even have gone further. In their group matches they drew with

Hungary, Mexico and Sweden and then in the quarter-final game lost 1-0 to the eventual winners, the newly resurgent Brazil, Pelé and all. Meanwhile in the 1-1 draw with Hungary Ivor had scored one of the greatest goals that many in the press box had every seen. Some thought him the best inside-forward in the whole tournament.

Ivor was one of the great stars of the 1950's: that was the decade in which he made his name and in which he had clearly become one of the adornments of the British game. Wearing the No. 10 shirt for Swansea Town and Wales he had become a truly national personality. His own particular hero, to whom he was to bear so much resemblance, was Peter Doherty, the red-haired Irish genius who came to fame with Derby County. Also in that Derby side which won the F.A. Cup was Raich Carter, another hugely skilful inside-forward with whom Allchurch was to be compared. Most teams had their elegant passers playing at inside-forward but obviously there was a hierarchy even for this collection of fifty or so master craftsmen. Clearly Ivor was already, in the 1950's, up there with the best. His name was only to be mentioned along with the greatest players like Doherty, Carter and Wilf Mannion of Middlesbrough who, week in and week out, proved that soccer artists, like great dancers, can be seen to defy the laws of physics by creating their own dimensions.

In the era of the maximum wage there was less incentive for stars to go in search of fame and fortune than in the later age of football millionaires and mercenaries but, all the same, most gifted players yearned to play regularly in front of the biggest and most knowledgeable crowds. What inspired ambition more that anything else was the sheer thought of having 70,000 fans cheering you every game, and that was what Everton, Manchester City, Arsenal and Spurs could offer. And what is more, playing for a glamour club increased one's chances of gaining the game's greatest honour, a Cup Final place in front of 100,000 at Wembley. 'He's bound to go', 'He's on his way', 'We'll never keep him': these were the comments made about all stars with small and unfashionable clubs. Well, Ivor stayed over ten years with the Swans before he signed for Newcastle United. Perhaps the transfer was just too late, for Newcastle were to go through a bad patch after their glory days earlier in the decade. Nevertheless, in a fading team Ivor became a great favourite playing in the famous black and white striped shirt in a St James Park, which was regularly filled with the most passionate, appreciative and knowledgeable crowds in

# IVOR IN DRAWING, TRADE CARD & CARICTURE

*Ivor in drawing, trade card and caricature.*

the whole British game. Ivor gave Newcastle four years of excellent service before returning to Wales to play club football at Ninian Park, Cardiff, a favourite ground of his, where he had so often displayed his skills for Wales. Bluebird fans soon grew to love this now ageing star from the past, and there were even those observers who thought that, although the hair was little more crinkled, Ivor was playing a sharper and more complete game than ever before. For Wales, too, he was better than ever.

Ivor was always a silent and undemonstrative man; he let his feet do all the talking. He was an exemplary footballer, a true gentleman in every respect. He was quite simply a footballing aristocrat. He aged as gracefully as he had always played. First it was back to the Vetch and then into non-league and Welsh League football. The repertoire was always the same: first the ball was controlled, then the body turned to shelter the ball and then came the oh-so-telling pass that invited his colleague to run on and do something special with the ball. Finally he did some coaching, urging boys to discipline their bodies, to remain athletes and then to make the ball do the work, all lessons he had learned from his father, his brothers and his Swansea teachers and coaches. He lived once more in his beloved Swansea, the city with which his name was now synonymous, a city which always claimed Dylan Thomas, the poet, as its most famous son, but which treasured the poetry of Ivor Allchurch, footballer, just as highly. Very clearly, he had loved to play for the Swans and what is more he had made the name of Swansea familiar wherever soccer was played. Who could ask for anything more? Entirely appropriately he was invested with the MBE in 1966. 'No player in modern times', commented Dewi Lewis, 'has done so much to lift the image of the professional game in Wales . . . he is the Stanley Matthews of Welsh Soccer'. But there was, of course, only one Ivor.

# CHAPTER ONE

# *Young Ivor's Swansea*

Joe Sykes turned up his collar against the slight drizzle. He had convinced himself that it would not come to much, for he was going to watch a match in which a young player who had been recommended to him was to appear. The match was to be played on the Cwm Level pitch, which was about two miles from Joe's home. It was September 1944. As was his habit, he set out to walk the distance, arriving in time to see the end of an under-16's match. The player in whom Sykes was interested was to play in the under-18's game which was to follow.

*The schoolboy Ivor.*

Joe Sykes had been captain of the Swansea Town side which had won the championship of Division Three (South) of the English League at the end of the 1924-5 season, and which had reached the semi final of the F.A. Cup a year later. He had been a cultured player, 'the doyen of the carpet passers', as the press of the day had it. He was a quiet, gentle man whose judgement of the potential of young players and whose skills in nurturing them were to prove to be outstanding. At the time, Joe was working as youth trainer and scout for the Swansea Town manager, Haydn Green.

As the under-16's left the pitch, Joe noticed a tall, spindly youth, who had been among those playing in the first match, talking to a man at the touchline. After a brief discussion, the boy took a jersey from the man, pulled it over his own and returned to the pitch, lining up at outside left. The circumstances surrounding this episode were, according to Joe Sykes in later years, to provide him with the greatest satisfaction of his life as a football scout. At the time, Joe gave little thought to the incident. It was not unusual in those wartime days for

*The boy footballer – August 1947.*

teams to be a man short, nor for them to recruit a substitute on the spot. What was different, Joe would recount, was the outstanding skill of the tall, blond substitute who caught and held the scout's attention throughout the game. The boy stood out amongst his seniors, and as Sykes had it, 'As soon as I saw his first touch I knew that I had unearthed a gem of rare quality'. That 'gem' was to become a legend in his own lifetime – the 'Golden Boy of Welsh Soccer', Ivor Allchurch, M.B.E.

Ivor's parents, Charlie and May Allchurch, were natives of Dudley in England's Black Country. In search of work for Charlie, in the middle of the recession, they had followed May's parents to Swansea. Initially they settled in the Waun Wen district of the town and, in view of the footballing prowess of their sons who were born there, that decision might be thought to be significant. Within a half-mile of their home, many other soccer internationals first saw the light of day. In their ranks were Jack Roberts (born 1918), Ernie Jones (born 1920), John Charles (born 1931), Mel Charles (born 1935), Trevor Ford (born 1923), and Mel Nurse (born 1937). Several English League professionals of good standing like Tom Kiley (born 1924) and Glyn Davies (born 1932) were also born in that area. When Ivor and Leonard Allchurch are added to that number, one can only stand amazed at the environment which produced such a crop of football talent within a single restricted district.

The young Allchurches grew up as part of a large family. There was step brother, Willie Miller, brothers Howard, Sid and Arthur, and sisters Evelyn and Dilys, plus Howard's daughter, Christine, who, following the death of her mother, was brought up by May. Together with Charlie and May, there were eleven of them living in a three bedroomed terraced house. It was an environment in which there had to be give and take. There was no room for prima donnas. In a footballing sense, however, there was a special atmosphere about the home. Charlie had played In the Birmingham League, Sid became a Welsh amateur international, whilst Arthur was a competent Welsh League player. In due course, the fact that the two babies of the family became full Welsh internationals was a matter of great rejoicing. However, as their personalities evolved and their footballing skills developed, that adoration was suitably masked so that the youngsters would, as the characteristic local idiom expressed it, 'grow up tidy'. And, grow up tidy they did, for as Bill Paton, a local journalist wrote when reporting on a London Combination match in which Ivor played following his demob:

17-year-old in London Combination action.

> 'Main interest . . . was centred in Ivor Allchurch, and knowing that Ivor will never need a large size in hats, let me say what a greatly improved player he is . . . Joe Sykes' faith in the lad has never been misplaced . . . he is going places.'

Ivor Williams, a close friend of Ivor's remembers that when the under-18's match at the Cwm Level pitch finished, two men went to speak to the youngster. The first was the man who had recruited the boy at the touchline. He shook Ivor's hand, ruffled his hair and gave him sixpence. The second turned out to be Joe Sykes, who was to become the 'Golden Boy's' mentor. Joe asked Ivor for his name and address and, during the following week, made his way to the Allchurch home at 39 Landeg Street in the Plasmarl district of Swansea. There, Joe obtained Charlie's agreement that, when the boy was fifteen, he would sign as an amateur for Swansea Town and train with them on Tuesdays and Thursdays. Had there been a ground staff at the time, it is probably that Ivor would have joined them. However, with the Vetch Field being used for military purposes, and wartime arrangements applying, this was not an option. Years later, Charlie was to say that he ought to have insisted that the boy be given an opportunity to learn a trade. At the time though, he confessed to being 'bursting with pride' and, anyway, he felt that Joe Sykes would look after his son. Joe did not disappoint him in that respect.

That Ivor Allchurch was born in a district of Swansea, which was a prolific cradle of special soccer talent, is a matter of record. Interestingly, though, the district to which the family moved – Plasmarl – was another of those Swansea 'villages' of the period which nurtured Welsh soccer greats. Among those who attended the same school as Ivor were Bobby Daniel, an Arsenal professional who was killed in the Second World War, and his brother Ray (Born 1928). And not too far away was the birthplace of Arsenal goalkeeper, Jack Kelsey (Born 1929). Given the overall record of Swansea for producing soccer talent at that time, it was hardly surprising that scouts from most major clubs were operating in the area.

From the age of eight, Ivor went to Plasmarl school and there came under the influence of Hugh Sinnett, a master with a particular interest in soccer. Mr Sinnett also ran the local youth club on three nights each week, and it was in teams representing this club that Ivor Allchurch began to develop as a footballer. Whilst it is right to give Joe Sykes great credit for finding and developing the youngster, an accolade is also due to Hugh Sinnett for the part which he played in the process. The point of particular interest is that, because of the War, schoolboy football was severely curtailed. Instead of the competitive inter-school Swansea league which had flourished before September 1939, only a handful of 'friendlies' were played by school sides. Hugh Sinnett's youth club helped to fill that void.

This was an important factor as far as Ivor's football development was concerned, and it also explains why the youngster did not obtain schoolboy honours. Whether he would have become an even better player had he done so can only be a matter of conjecture. Certainly, the boy would have graced an eleven produced even by a remarkable Swansea schools organisation which developed outstanding teams in the years immediately before and after the Second World War. During that period the Town's schoolboys won the English Schools Shield on no fewer than four occasions, playing a brand of exciting football which was the envy of other towns and cities. Such was their appeal that they attracted crowds of 20,000 and more on a regular basis. Cliff Jones, John Charles, Terry Medwin and Len Allchurch were among the cadre of outstanding internationals-to-be which Swansea schools produced in those years. Whilst there is little doubt that he would have lived with such talent, Ivor was either too young or too old to have been part of the scene.

A second feature of the Sinnett-Allchurch relationship was that, typically of non-academic boys of that era, Ivor left school at fourteen. Consequently it was left to Mr Sinnett's youth club to provide a continuing influence which might otherwise have been diminished. Whilst the club was not concerned with the 'Three Rs', it embraced the disciplines and ethos which were typical of Welsh education of the time. That fitted with the Allchurch family philosophy and with the persistent culture of the working class society in which the club was set. Then, when Ivor went to join Joe Sykes at fifteen, it is probable that he saw it simply as a continuation of the process within which he had been nurtured. If that is true, it is not surprising that, even when he was a seasoned Welsh international he continued to refer to his mentor as Mr Sykes.

When Ivor left school he was found a job in the office at Baldwins Foundry, where they made bomb casings. He didn't enjoy the work, and was about to ask his father if he could try something else, when he stumbled across a solution. One winter's afternoon, on his way home from work, he saw a group of his friends playing football on a local park. When he enquired how they could be doing that, one of them, Derek Thomas, told him that it was because they worked in the Fish Market. It seemed that, in wartime winter, the market often closed

*Boy amongst men . . . Frank Barson pep talk, pre-season 1947-8.*

early because of a lack of fish. As a result, the lads who worked there were released around one p.m. Not surprisingly, Ivor was attracted to a job, which would allow him to play even more football. Consequently, when another fish porter was 'called up', Derek recommended his pal as a replacement, and the young Allchurch began a job which he did until signing for Swansea Town in 1947. Not that May Allchurch wanted him to work there, for she had a premonition that he would fall into the dock – which he did.

Like most mothers of the era, May Allchurch knew her children well, though, according to Derek Thomas, she, and his own mother would have been mortified had they known of some of the schoolboy exploits in which they were involved. Nothing was too daring for the boys to try. Among many hair-raising activities in which they engaged were, sliding down a steep coal tip on a sheet of rusting corrugated iron, careering down a steep hill on a home-made bike without brakes, swimming in a stagnant canal, and climbing over the glass-topped wall of the local scrap yard to find components for bikes and trolleys.

And, like other boys of their generation and environment, they had to 'look after themselves'. In that respect, Derek Thomas remembers Ivor being goaded by a lad who fancied himself as the local pugilist. When all else failed, the ten year-old Allchurch was forced to defend himself when attacked by the other boy. Whilst boxing was hardly his forte, his friends were surprised to see him standing up, unflinchingly, to the blows which he received. And when the other lad tired, Ivor turned the tables. From that day forward, Ivor Allchurch was held in great esteem by the boys of the neighbourhood as a 'tough guy', though no one can remember seeing him fight again.

Yet, however tough he was, one element of the rewards of the fish market job tells us much about another aspect of Ivor's personality. Each employee at the market was allowed to augment his wages once a week by taking home some fish, which he could sell. So shy was Ivor that younger brother, Len, was delegated to do the selling. In return, Ivor treated Len and sister, Dilys to a weekly visit to a local cinema. That shyness remained with Ivor throughout his life and was hardly diminished by fame. Whilst it was an appealing aspect of his make-up, it also served to frustrate some who did not have the opportunity to get to know him well. Some fellow players and several journalists came into this category.

Perhaps, in part, this explains why no one has produced a biography of Ivor before. Certainly, because of his innate shyness he was not easy to interview. He was reluctant to talk about himself even though, like most people, he enjoyed being spoken and written about. In addition to his shyness though, there was another factor which caused him to be cautious about journalists. He loved the game of football and he had an abhorrence of those who wished to besmirch soccer with tales of avarice and corruption. He told his friend Ivor Williams on three occasions that he had been approached about writing a book, 'but all they seem to want is dirt'. Being 'brought up tidy' encompassed decent behaviour, loyalty and a reluctance to speak ill of others. Such things were the norm in the Allchurch household and were reinforced by the guidance of Messrs. Sinnett and Sykes.

Not surprisingly, Ivor's pride in his elder brothers' prowess on the football field was another influence. He watched them play and learnt from them the necessity to practice skills which 'gave you time on the ball'. That was one of the reasons why the pine end of Mrs Davies's corner shop was peppered with tennis ball marks. Brother Len remembers spending hours using this wall as a training aid; trapping, shooting, heading, a thousand times over. Any open piece of ground served the same purpose, and matches of twenty plus on each side were played (with coats as goals) until the light failed, whilst, as often, two or three practiced their footballing skills in some corner of a field. In fact, in Ivor's case, May Allchurch's admonition of him when he was guilty of some minor misdemeanor was very near the truth. 'All you think of is football!'

Thinking about football became a way of life for the tall, blond boy when he arrived at the Vetch Field and became absorbed into a wider football family. There, he worked hard at his training and playing. To some degree he was in awe of the senior professionals at the Vetch, but quickly settled down under the guidance of Joe Sykes into a pattern of life which, to his young mind, was idyllic. Now, he was absorbed in football morning, noon and night.

During the period when he was an amateur at the Vetch Field, on two separate occasions, scouts from other English League teams tried to persuade Ivor to sign for them when he became sixteen. Each time he refused, saying that he and his father had given their word that he would sign for Swansea Town. A Leeds scout, however, who had a closer relationship with Swansea, was more successful with John Charles, who had joined the groundstaff after Ivor. Indeed, he took Charles and several other boys to Leeds in a clandestine move which was to result in a change in the rules regarding ground staff boys. Whilst only Charles signed for the Yorkshire club, his immense talent was lost to Swansea Town. The Vetch authorities argued at the time that there was an implicit agreement that their groundstaff boys would sign for the club when they became sixteen. Sadly for them, the letter of the law which applied then had it that, until their sixteenth birthday, boys were free agents and could join any club of their choice. Whilst the rules were changed subsequently so as to give the host club tenure over the youngsters, in John Charles's case the damage had been done. Had Ivor and Charlie Allchurch not adopted the stance which they did, another outstanding talent would have been lost to Swansea Town.

At the beginning of Ivor's sojourn at the Vetch his elder brothers were away in the forces. This left Charlie to watch developments and report to the older boys in his letters. However, whenever the 'big brothers' were home on leave they would cast their eye over the youngsters in whatever match was being played. This practice per-sisted for many years as Ivor developed and, in due course they would go to the Vetch Field to see him play for the Reserves. On many occasions, on arriving home they would dissect his game and tell him what he should or should not have done. Indeed, this persisted even after he had become a fixture in the Swans' first team. He would listen but not comment, until one day, with a quiet smile he said, 'I tell you what, you go and do it next week.' The smiles all round put the criticism into perspective though, as Ivor said, 'It was all meant for my good and they *were* good footballers!'

From what has been written here the reader will have gained an insight into the personality and character of Ivor John Allchurch. In many ways these factors influenced his development both as a person and a footballer, but it is not the intention here to try to analyse the impact of those influences on the man. Nor is it to contrast the brash confidence of many present day 'stars' with Ivor's retiring demeanour. Not only was Ivor a child of his family environment, he was also one of the mores and social environment of his day. Then, truly great players like Tom Finney and Stanley Matthews didn't need agents and press conferences to tell the world how good they were. Like them, Ivor Allchurch was brought up to believe that his feet should do the talking. As we shall see, they certainly did that.

CHAPTER TWO

# Footballer, Soldier and Professional

Like the majority of young men of his generation, on reaching his
eighteenth birthday in 1948, Ivor was required to serve King and
country. In his case he was enlisted in the Army, ostensibly as a Gunner.
In effect, though, once his prowess was recognised, he spent much of
his time playing football. Based at Oswestry, he represented his unit,
his corps, Western Command and the Army, in addition to 'guesting'
for Shrewsbury Town, and Wellington Town (now Telford United).
Indeed, during the football season, it was not unusual for him to play
three matches each week which, together with training sessions, required the Army authorities to be 'flexible' with respect to his duties
as a soldier.

*Western Command XI, 1948-9.*

In the process, and as a result of the general Army training regime, Ivor developed physically whilst becoming fitter than he had ever been. In addition, as a result of playing with other young soccer professionals who were serving with him, he was able to hone his skills, and mature as a footballer perhaps more quickly than normally might have been expected. Ivor believed that, although some people looked upon National Service as a waste of time, it provided him with a beneficial opportunity. He was convinced that this physical fitness, combined with Army discipline and many opportunities to play football at a good level, helped him to develop in many ways. 'Square bashing', assault courses and the rest were all taken in his stride, for his boyhood experiences had prepared him for the challenges which he now encountered.

When Ivor played for Western Command in November 1948, he was spotted by Leslie Knighton, the manager of Shrewsbury Town, who, within a matter of days had signed the youngster to play for his club. Knighton recalled that he thought that he had 'found a future star', but was not surprised to be told that the young soldier was on the books of an English League club. He said that Ivor had 'vision and a lovely touch', and that he 'bossed the games in which he played'.

Before joining the Army, Ivor had cut his teeth as a footballer in the physically exacting environment of the Welsh League. Starting as a sixteen year old he played against teams from the valley mining towns, which, in many instances, were made up of a mixture of old professionals and hard-as-nails miners. As a result, he needed to 'look after himself' on the football field. Certainly, those games were not for the faint hearted. 'Heavy pitches, heavy balls and heavy tackles', was how one observer described them, and for a spindly sixteen year old, they provided testing challenges week by week. Tommy Farr used to point to his 'schooling' in the boxing booths of his younger days. Ivor's 'booths' were those Welsh League games.

With such experience behind him, he was prepared for anything he came up against in the matches in which he played during his service years. Undoubtedly, the better surfaces on which he performed proved to be beneficial to his game, and, if he was faced with robust play, he was able to deal with it. As a consequence, he fitted well into the Shrewsbury set-up at the time, and became something of a favourite with the club's supporters. He made his début at Gay Meadow on 20 November 1948 and played for the club throughout the remainder of that season.

*Soldier Ivor greets bigwig with Wellington Town, 1949-50.*

For the 1949-50 campaign, though, Ivor transferred his allegiance to Wellington Town, and played for that club until he was demobbed. At Wellington, Ivor lined up against the reserve sides of clubs like Wrexham, Stockport County and Tranmere Rovers, which provided him with further useful experience. This was enhanced by the representative matches he played for Army sides.

The reporter of the local paper which covered the Wellington matches, was clearly taken with the play of the young soldier. 'Old Sport', reporting on a match against Tranmere Reserves, used the headline 'Allchurch Star of the game'. Ivor, it seemed, was 'his usual clever self'. Then, in the journalist's report of a match against the Wrexham reserve side he wrote: 'The ball came across from the right and Allchurch, running in, flashed it into the net before it reached the ground', and 'For clever ball-manipulation the palm goes to Allchurch. This young player has a touch of class about him which stamps him as a future star.'

In the course of time many astute judges would agree with the reporter's judgement. The ball manipulation and the fierce volleying were to be appreciated on many football grounds around the world. Had they but known it, the spectators watching those Wellington Town games during that 1949-50 season were being treated to a privileged preview of a world-class player in embryo.

When Ivor returned to the Vetch Field following his demob, he came with glowing recommendations from knowledgeable observers who had watched his progress through those end-of-the-decade seasons. Among them was the Shrewsbury manager, Leslie Knighton, who said that he turned away 'dozens of enquiries from First Division clubs, on the grounds that 'we don't own him'. Knighton, who described Allchurch as a 'second Charlie Buchan', had passed the enquiries to the Swansea manager, Billy McCandless. The latter confirmed that he had received substantial offers from big clubs for the boy, but that he didn't intend to sell. Given that, at the time, Allchurch had still not made his English League début, this interest caused much discussion at the Vetch Field. One man who was not surprised by it all, was Joe Sykes.

*1949-50*

Nevertheless, Ivor found that, despite these enthusiastic recommendations, he was required to resume his full time career at the Vetch Field in the club's reserve side – which played in the London Combination. Apart from anything else, after carrying all before them, the Swansea club had been promoted as champions of Division Three (South) at the end of the previous campaign. In the process the side had won twenty-seven of its English League matches, had been beaten only seven times and had not lost at home. They had scored eighty-seven goals whilst conceding only thirty-four, and inside forwards, McCrory and Lucas had played in all but a handful of games. Lucas was a Welsh international, and McCrory's play was to result in his being 'capped' by Northern Ireland. In addition, conventional wisdom at the Vetch Field at the time held it that young players should be 'nursed in case they burned themselves out'.

A consequence of all this was that Ivor was not considered for first team selection until the Christmas period 1949. In those days, it was usual for teams to play three games in the four days which included Christmas Day and Boxing Day. As a result, it was common practice to rest some of the older legs and bring in reserve players and Ivor was given his chance that day, and did enough to satisfy the Swansea management that he was ready for first team football. Not that any of the players were surprised. As Terry Elwell, the Swansea Town left back that day, recalled: 'I remember the first time I met Ivor. It was before a reserve match at the Vetch Field, and when the players went into the dressing room we found a blond youth dressed in an Army uniform sitting there alone. The reserve team captain went to speak to the youngster, then introduced him to the others: "This is the Ivor Allchurch we've heard so much about." Nobody said much then, but, at the end of the match every one of the Swansea players went to shake the young man's hand. We were hooked on Ivor Allchurch from then on!'

Ivor was rested for the match on the following day, but recalled for the F.A. Cup-tie against Birmingham City at the Vetch Field on 7 January 1950. Thereafter the name 'Allchurch, I.' became a fixture at inside left on the Swansea Town team sheet. No one suggested that the youngster would 'burn out'.

It was during that game with Birmingham City that Ivor really caught the attention of the media for the first time. Whilst Birmingham were not doing well at the time, they *were* a First Division team and included several excellent players in their side, including the England goal keeper, Gil Merrick. But the Birmingham men could not match Swansea, who won the match comfortably, and Allchurch was one of the names on the score sheet, a fact not lost on the Swansea supporters. But it was a match in the next round which 'lit the blue touch paper' and launched the career of Ivor Allchurch into orbit.

Swansea were drawn to play Arsenal at Highbury, and the star-studded 'Gunners' side was installed as firm favourite to win comfortably. In the event they were desperately hard-pressed to justify that confidence. 57,305 people were packed into Highbury, with the Swansea contingent numbering less than 7,000, yet, at the end, the sporting majority acclaimed the men in white, particularly their blond inside left. The man delegated to mark Ivor in that match was Scottish international, Alex Forbes, but, before the end of an enthralling contest, as the youngster worked his magic, Joe Mercer, left half in the Arsenal middle line, had to support the Scot on several occasions. Indeed, on one occasion, after beating Forbes, the Swansea man seemed to mesmerise Mercer, prostrate on the ground, to the extent that, when the ball drifted out of play, Joe reached out and grabbed Ivor's ankle.

His smile as he did so spoke volumes. Ivor Allchurch had arrived on the big stage!

In a speech to a Swansea Sportsmen's club many years later, Joe Mercer, remembering the incident, paid tribute to the Swansea team and, in particular to Ivor Allchurch. 'You nearly frightened us to death,' he said. Every commentator following that memorable Highbury game echoed Joe's words. Most said that the Swans were unlucky not to have drawn the match at least, and by implication, if nothing else, that they were lucky to have such a player as Allchurch in their ranks. Yet the game had been only Ivor's fifth first-team match and his first against a top side. And the 'Gunners' who went on to win the F.A. Cup that season, *were* one of the country's major sides at the time, and included players like Barnes, Swindin, Logie, and Leslie Compton.

In the press coverage of the game, the sports writers, to a man, forecast that one or more of the big clubs would be knocking on Swansea's door to snap up Ivor Allchurch for a 'fee which could not be refused'. Indeed, in the week which followed, several first-division clubs were rumoured to have made bids for the player. But, manager McCandless and his chairman kept stressing that the player was not for sale. Not that that stopped further speculation and, on the following Saturday, when Swansea went to play Luton at Kenilworth Road, it was said that the home club had difficulty in finding seats for all the scouts who wished to attend the match. Predictably, the Press Corps was out in force that day to report on the new sensation. And they were not disappointed! The Swans won by two goals to one, but there was only one name of everybody's lips – Ivor Allchurch, number ten.

Many column inches were filled in his praise in the week that followed, but Alex James, the old Arsenal forward, summed up the comments of many when he wrote:

'Tom Whittaker was at Luton watching players . . . but I should imagine that, like everyone else, he had eyes for only one player long before the match finished. It was a great triumph for young Ivor Allchurch, the Swansea inside-left.

This tall youngster, with the hair of Peter Doherty, and the same fighting spirit, too, has a body swerve like David Jack, and drags the ball and his foot over it just like another Ronnie Starling.

. . . The money bags will be jingling over the weekend.'

Whilst the Swansea telephone was busier than usual in the week which followed, so were the legion of former players who commented in the football sections of the nation's newspapers, and those who filled the press benches. As a result, flattering descriptions of young Ivor were printed by the score, but none surpassed a comment credited to the Arsenal manger, Tom Whittaker. Whittaker, who was among the men trying to persuade Swansea to sell, gave a whole new meaning to the word hyperbole when he said: 'I regard Ivor Allchurh as the player of the Century.'

At the time, there were those who felt that the Arsenal man had overstated his case, but no one was prepared to argue other than that the 'Welsh Wizard', as one press man had labelled Ivor, had 'arrived'. He had, unquestionably, made a remarkable impact upon the football world; an impact so startling that no one seemed able to cite its equal for such a young player in the recent history of the game.

At the Vetch Field, however, Ivor found himself to be a member of a side which was struggling to make an impact on Division Two. Despite having been so successful during the previous season, and although they were regularly including as many as seven internationals in the team, results left much to be desired. It was clear to most observers that the team needed strengthening, but the Swansea board declared that they 'did not intend to speculate'. It was a stance which, in due course, resulted in Ivor and other key players leaving the club. At the time, though, there was some comfort for Swansea supporters in that the club's chairman announced that they were not going to sell their better players either. And, in that regard, much was made of their refusal of 'record bids' from Arsenal and Liverpool, amongst others, for Ivor Allchurch and Roy Paul. The board declared that they intended to 'develop their own talent', and, 'build on what we have here'.

Sadly, 'what they had' was diminished soon after by serious injury to Irish internationals O'Driscoll and Keane, and the available replacements did not match up to the demands of the Second Division. Then, later in the season, in a move which angered Swansea supporters, the club sold Jim Feeney and Sam McCrory to Ipswich Town, thereby intensifying the difficulties which the team faced.

Whilst Ivor was too new to the game to form judgements about good and bad football management, he was aware of the disappointment of his team mates. A line from a Louis Armstrong song seemed to the players to sum up the Swansea board's attitude: 'They ain't got no ambition.' Ivor remembered Roy Paul grumbling about the decision, and felt that Roy's disappointment was one of the reasons why he went to Bogotá and, subsequently, to Manchester City.

From Ivor's point of view, though, having only recently come home from the Army, the last thing he wanted to do was move. There was also the question of romance. He had become secretly engaged to sixteen-year old Esme whose parents, although happy for her and Ivor to be friends, were not willing for the relationship 'to get too serious'. Esme, they said, had to wait until she was eighteen before becoming engaged. At the time such decisions were rarely challenged, so, had Ivor been transferred, the couple felt that they would be separated. Neither wanted that to happen. Consequently, when Joe Sykes urged Ivor to 'hang on we've got some great youngsters coming through,' he was inclined to believe him.

Furthermore, whatever disappointment was felt by the players and supporters at the Vetch Field, at the end of his first (part) season in the English League, Ivor could look back on a remarkable four months. He had established himself in the Swansea side, had attracted much praise from knowledgeable observers of the game, and had been the subject of what were then regarded as breathtaking offers by other clubs. There were rumours, too, that the F.A. of Wales had noted his performances with interest. Some might have argued that such talk was premature, but Ivor felt that what had already happened to him was beyond all his expectations. Anything seemed to be possible! In addition, he found himself the proud owner of a Welsh Cup winners' medal, having played a significant part in the defeat of Wrexham at Cardiff. He was encouraged, too, by the success of the latest Swansea Schools' side and by the progress being made by young stars on the club's groundstaff. What Joe Sykes had said made a great deal of sense; and, of course, there was Esme.


*1950-1*


In July 1950 when Roy Paul left the Vetch to join Manchester City for a fee of £25,000, the concerns which had dismayed the players and supporters during the previous season were resurrected. The Swansea directors made much of the fact that Paul had insisted on a move and that, even though he had returned to the Vetch after walking out on them to go to Bogotá , they felt that it was better to part company with the player. The staff at the Vetch and the long-suffering supporters could do little but accept the situation. Indeed, such was the air of inevitability abroad in the town that, had Ivor been transferred at that time, the news would have been received with numb resignation.

Deepening the gloom, early results in the new season did little to provide anyone with comfort. After five matches, only one point had been gained, and manager McCandless had demonstrated his concern by making frequent team changes. Yet, throughout that grey period, young Allchurch was a fixture in the side. Initially, he played at inside left, then at inside-right. However, for a match at home to Doncaster on 2 September he reverted to number ten. There he remained for the rest of the season and in so doing he set a club record as the youngest player ever to have been 'ever present' during an English League campaign.

Not that the feat surprised his mentor, Joe Sykes. Joe was of the opinion that such were Ivor's balance and poise that he was 'more likely to steer clear of injury,' whilst 'avoiding the scything tackles of cloggers'. Meanwhile, Frank Barson, the Swansea trainer and self-styled 'hard man', said that 'Ivor was tougher than he looked', and that he was 'one of the greatest inside forwards in the four countries.' There was general agreement about the latter statement, whilst, had he been asked, Ivor's boyhood pal, Derek Thomas, could have confirmed the former.

Despite Swansea's lack of success, interest continued in the possibility of other clubs signing the 'Welsh Wizard'. Wolverhampton, Liverpool and Manchester City were among those said to have made substantial offers for the player. But, still, the Swansea board stood firm. In addition, manager McCandless was allowed to bring in some new faces, though, sadly, these players reflected both the small fees involved and the manger's lack of success as a buyer. Nonetheless, he was boosted by the burgeoning promise of some of the youngsters in the care of Joe Sykes. During what was a difficult season, McCandless blooded future internationals like Terry Medwin and Johnny King; players like Harry Griffiths, another Welsh 'cap' to-be, were due for demob in the not-too-distant future; and Ivor's brother Len, and Cliff Jones were others on the horizon. The trouble was, of course, that despite the tremendous promise of these lads, the club could have done with them there and then.

As far as Ivor was concerned his development appeared to be un-affected by his playing in an unsuccessful side. Indeed, rumours began circulating that the twenty-year-old would be 'capped' against England at Sunderland in the November of 1950. Those rumours proved to be well-founded and, despite having only played thirty English League matches, Ivor won his first 'cap' on the fifteenth of that month. Now, the critics argued, he would be really tested by players of the highest calibre. And the English team was formidable, and included players like: Williams, Ramsey, Dickinson, Finney, Mannion, and Milburn.

Willie Watson, also an international cricketer, a player of the no-nonsense school, was to mark Ivor. Joe Sykes told his charge to forget about the opposition and play his normal game. He did that and, with-out setting the world on fire, in the eyes of most critics he enhanced his growing reputation. Roy Paul, playing behind Ivor that day, wrote later: '. . . we saw Bryn Jones's place brilliantly filled; Ivor Allchurch, then only just twenty-one, showed himself to be an inside left stamped with a real mark of greatness.'

*The Times* reported: 'The opening England goal . . . was . . . not a moment too soon, for Wales, with Allchurch and Clarke, in particular worrying Ramsey and Watson in defence, were going from strength to strength . . . Wales had clearly worried their opponents in that first half hour, with Allchurch in particular showing rich promise.'

Swansea supporters, although delighted to read such comments about their new young star, could not help feeling that Ivor had been put on display in yet another shop window. Surely, they thought, now that he had proved himself at international level, some big club would snatch him away in return for a fat fee. But it was not to be . . . not for some time anyway.

What no one at the time could have known was that the quality of that début performance was to be repeated on the international stage on numerous occasions thereafter. Indeed, that match in which he won his first 'cap' was to be the first of twenty-seven consecutive games which Ivor was to play for Wales during the next six seasons. It was a remarkable record for a relatively young player, and was to pro-vide the foundation for the-then record-breaking sixty-eight 'caps' which Ivor won over sixteen years. Joe Sykes, never had any doubts on that score. His 'gem of rare quality' had fulfilled all the promise he had shown on that public pitch in war-time Swansea.

Meantime, in the Swansea shirt, during the disappointing 1950-1 season, Allchurch continued to baffle the opposition, charm the fans, and attract scouts like bees to a hive. It seemed that the press corps turned out *en masse* wherever he played, and in a match against Leicester which Swansea won by three goals to two they were running out of superlatives to describe the young maestro's game. 'Astounding', 'Mesmerising', 'Magical', 'Effortless conjuring' and 'Slide-rule passing' were among those used by different journalists. In the report in the local Swansea paper, the writer took the opportunity to drop a broad hint to the Vetch board 'there stands out the defence-splitting efforts of a wizard with the ball – Allchurch. How foolish the club would be to part with such a player as part of any transfer deal.' Two weeks later Ivor captured most of the headlines again with a masterly display against Bury. Whilst both clubs were in the relegation zone at the time, Ivor, according to most papers, was 'head and shoulders above the rest.' One journalist described him as: 'An Association football artist on a green-brown canvas who painted a picture worthy of an Old master.' It was hardly Pulitzer prize material, but reflected faithfully the feelings of the growing band of fans who found Ivor's display to be inspirational.

Sadly, though, one man cannot make a team, and even Ivor's brilliance could not stem the flow of defeats which followed that match. So desperate was the situation that, at the end of February, the Swansea board, fearing the threat of relegation, finally allowed McCandless to spend a reasonable amount of money on a player. He bought Ronnie Turnbull from Manchester City. Turnbull, an experienced centre-forward proved his worth by scoring eight goals in the thirteen matches which remained. At the end of the season on being congratulated on his efforts, he was quick to praise Ivor and his part in the process: 'With a player like Ivor alongside you, many chances come your way.' Allchurch himself also played a part in the goal-scoring which heralded a mini-revival in the club's fortunes. He scored in four consecutive matches.

Given the form of the team during the last weeks of the season, there were those who forecast that the next campaign would see the Swansea club challenging for promotion. From where Ivor Allchurch stood, that seemed a reasonable assessment of the situation. Furthermore, Joe Sykes was enthusing about the young players who were 'coming through'. Terry Medwin, Cliff Jones, Harry Griffiths, Mel Charles and young Len were all going to make the 'big time'. 'Wait,'

*First team footballer, 1952.*
*Back row: T. Elwell, R. Turnbull, R. Keane, J. King, K. Clarke, G. Beech.*
*Front row: T. Medwin, W. Lucas, R. Weston, I. Allchurch, A. Bellis.*

said Joe, 'until these boys line up with you.' For the fans the prospect
was mouth-watering.

The 1951-2 season provided Ivor with further opportunities to em-
bellish his footballing c.v. In September he was selected to play for the
Welsh League against the Irish League, which, although not having
the cachet of a full international, provided another stage upon which
the twenty-one year old could perform his wizardry. And he did that,
scoring two and 'making' three in a match in which his skills shone
like a lighthouse at midnight.

At outside left in the Welsh side that day was experienced international, George Edwards. Later in his life, Edwards remembered Ivor
beating three men before slipping the ball to the unmarked winger,
who scored. The Windsor Park faithful, as so many crowds of the era
had done, applauded the blond youngster back to the centre circle.
Edwards said that it was like a theatre curtain call. The maestro had

won another set of adherents; yet Ivor's only response was to touch Edward's hand by way of acknowledgement. It was the beauty of his football which won the hearts of the crowds – even if their own side suffered in the process .

And this was witnessed by London journalists when they went to Loftus Road to cover the Q.P.R. versus Swansea match. The superlatives flowed yet again. One reporter wrote: 'It is probable that there have been more . . . .transfer offers for Ivor Allchurch . . . than for any other young player. Watching him . . . it was easy to appreciate why this young man with the educated feet has reached his present position . . .' And: 'Swansea are fortunate in being able to include in their attack one of the greatest of Britain's . . . forwards . . . The equaliser – a free kick that Allchurch fired home like a rocket – was worth the admission money to see.'

Once again, the hallmarks of Ivor's play were there for the scribes to enjoy. 'Brilliance on the ball' was one thing, but when that was combined with lethal shooting with either foot, they knew that they were in the presence of an extraordinary player.

When Swansea's English League season came to a close, pre-season optimism had vanished and the side finished in 19th place in the division, one notch lower than at the end of the previous campaign. By then, Ivor was becoming restless. When playing at international level he was, constantly, being urged by his team mates to move to a first-division club. They argued that he would be an even greater player as a result of regular competition at the top level. But McCandless and Sykes once again urged Ivor to bide his time. The outstanding youngsters they had spoken about were 'coming through', and there was no reason why Ivor could not be playing first-division football at the Vetch Field. It was what Ivor wanted to believe and, as he said at the time, there was no financial advantage in leaving Swansea.

He also allowed himself to be encouraged by the progress which the club had made in the F.A. Cup. After beating Reading at Elm Park, the Swans disposed of Rotherham at the Vetch to reach the last sixteen in the competition. The victory over Rotherham, by three clear goals, was hailed as an Allchurch win. The headlines told the tale: 'Allchurch wizardry'; 'Mr Magic again'; 'Rotherham in an Allchurch daze'; and 'Allchurch supreme'. One report had it that, 'The Yorkshire defence reacted like somnambulists against the inspired trickery of Ivor Allchurch', while another paper reported that 'The wizardry of

Allchurch bemused the Rotherham defence.' It was vintage Ivor, even if the wine was rather young.

Nevertheless, there were those who were sounding a cautionary note about Ivor's progress, though nothing of that appeared in the reports from the Vetch Field regarding the next round tie with the mighty Newcastle United. At the time Newcastle was the glamour side of English football. Jackie Milburn, the Robledo brothers, Frank Brennan, Joe Harvey and Ron Simpson were among their stars. They were the favourites to take the F.A. Cup, and second-division Swansea were given little chance of beating them. In the event those who were at the Vetch field that day saw an exciting, evenly matched game which Newcastle managed to win by virtue of a single Bobby Mitchell goal. After the game, all agreed that the Swansea men, particularly Allchurch, had done enough to warrant a replay at least. Had it not been, they said, for the brilliance of Simpson in goal and the superb defending of Frank Brennan, Swansea might have scored three. The volume of applause at the end of the match, for both sides, said it all, and it was noticeable how many Newcastle men went to shake the hand of Ivor Allchurch. As Alf McMichael admitted 'We were lucky to get away with it!' As far as Ivor was concerned, his performance resurrected the rumours about other clubs signing him. Newcastle, themselves, and Manchester United were said to be in discussions with Swansea about buying their number ten. To the Swansea fans the signs were gloomily ominous. And, by then, there were those among the supporters who, albeit grudgingly, acknowledged that it would be in the player's interest to join a big club.

As Ivor said later, 'At that time I was beginning to believe that I should go.' Journalist, Scottie Hall, had no doubt that he ought. His comments were cutting: 'I saw Ivor Allchurch playing for Wales against Scotland . . . He scored a memorable goal from long distance. This was a goal that saved Allchurch from being a Hampden flop . . . (he) scarcely hinted at the greatness with which he was being freely labelled just a season ago . . . Through my binoculars . . . Allchurch . . . (is) suffering because of the lack of adequate challenge . . . (he) needs the stimulus of valid competition, and (he) is not getting it.'

Ivor's fervent fans might have rejected these comments as nonsense, but Hall's words were telling enough to make the footballer himself carefully paste the article in his scrap book.

# CHAPTER 3

# *A Man of Wales*

The World Cup year of 1998 was a sad one for Welsh Football and, perhaps, for Ryan Giggs in particular. The Manchester United winger was generally regarded as one of the most talented players in the English Premiership – if not in Europe – and yet he was unable to display his talent in a World Cup tournament which could have done with his exhilarating pace and attacking flair. Not only in Wales but throughout the United Kingdom soccer-lovers bemoaned the absence of Giggs, and comments were made on the contrasting experiences of Giggs and England's new superstar, Michael Owen. Giggs brought up in Manchester, had yet opted to play for Wales, the country of his birth; Owen, who had lived all his life in Wales, was born in Chester and wisely perhaps opted for England. Once again there was speculation as to whether there should be a United Kingdom or Great Britain team. Certainly there was in Wales a sense of shame; Giggs had been let down by a soccer nation that in that World Cup year had not only failed to qualify for the finals, but was not even rated among the world's top one hundred soccer countries.

Ryan Giggs was not the first world-class player to be denied football's major showcase because of his Welsh nationality. In recent years, other supremely talented players like Ian Rush, Neville Southall and Mark Hughes had not been given the opportunity to play in the finals of major national championships. There had been some near misses and even moments of glory, such as a win against Germany, but generally it was thought that Wales tended to rely too heavily on a handful of stars and always had areas of weakness, especially in mid-field and defence. Yet there was often a degree of optimism and the certainty of pride.

That pride had much to do with tradition. Wales; after all had played its first international game as long ago as 1876, the first against England had come in 1881, and in Billy Meredith, Wales had produced the first British super-star, the forerunner of George Best, Paul Gascoigne and Ryan Giggs.

*'A back for Fordy" . . . training with Wales, 1951.*

Welsh club soccer, like everything else in the Principality, suffered in the Depression, but the national side had done much to sustain morale amongst those both in and out of work. The Home International Championship was the vital arena for national aspirations. Wales won it three times in the 1920's and four times in the 1930's. That championship served to give Welsh stars an international measure and also allowed supporters at home to appraise famous players like Bryn Jones, who then, invariably, played their club football in England. There were great memories and indeed legends from pre-1914 and pre-1939 days, but nothing really to compare with what happened late in the 1950's. These were to be the 'Golden Years' of British football, and they were the years that generated a pride in the Welsh team that has served as the basis of national soccer identity to this day. This was the team for which Ivor Allchurch made his début in 1950.

In the new post-war culture the masses wanted to be entertained as never before. In their millions they went to cinemas and sports arenas wanting the very best. In every sphere of popular culture expectations were enormous. Now that soccer was better supported and more fully reported than ever before, the people of Wales wanted to see their team take up where they had left off at the end of the Thirties. Every year they wanted to see the Home Championship won and in particular they longed for success against England. Those things were initially to prove elusive, but there were pleasing compensations. In this new age of mass interest, both the fans and the press were eager to acclaim the charismatic players who had personality and genius. These were the years when Matthews, Finney, Lawton and Carter were dominating the headlines. If Wales was to hold its own in this new soccer environment, it, too, needed a new generation of stars.

Pre-war stars like Bryn Jones and Tommy Jones were still in the team in the early post-war years, but attention was now switching to the search for new men. Mercifully there was a new cohort of class defenders, players whose names would be filled-in automatically on the team sheet for years to come. Walley Barnes, a north Londoner fortuitously born in Brecon, was the most intelligent of full-backs; alongside him was Aberaman's Alf Sherwood who was to develop into one of the game's most fearsome tacklers, so much so that it was said that Matthews in particular always thought twice about the wisdom of playing against Cardiff City and Wales. In front of them and playing on either side of Tommy Jones were two complete half-backs, Roy

Paul and the magisterial Ronnie Burgess, both sons of the mining valleys, who were respected throughout the land for their leadership, work-rate and their ability to switch from defence to attack.

For years these men provided Wales with a solid base, but more was needed if a successful side was to be established. Outstanding defenders were all very well, but it was forwards who always stole the headlines as match-winners. In the first post-war internationals the number 9 shirt was handed to Swansea Town's Trevor Ford and Welsh soccer was given a new dimension. In those post-war years Ford introduced a thrill factor into the national game. He was small for a centre-forward but he had every other qualification for that most exciting of positions. He was dark and handsome and always made things happen. Later, after Aston Villa had paid £10,000 for his services, Welsh soccer fans took great pride in his goals for the Midland side, for Sunderland and Wales. If the national team was ever to achieve success rather than respect, then surely Ford would be the cutting edge. However, the country's most expensive player needed support.

It was an age of outstanding inside-forwards. They were the great intellects and magicians of football, and Wales needed to have such men. Not since the pre-war days of Bryn Jones at his best, and of Dai Astley, had Wales been up to scratch in this respect. Consequently, in November 1950, when the 21 year-old Ivor Allchurch played his first game for his country against England at Roker Park, Sunderland, and was an immediate success, there was great rejoicing in the Welsh camp. The wait for a quality inside-forward was over! That day, in a very good game which England won 4-2, Ford scored twice but had to share the headlines with Allchurch, who was adjudged 'one of the outstanding personalities of the game'. Even at that time his senior team-mates, such as Barnes and Paul, were talking of his 'greatness', and quite naturally, there was greatly increased speculation as to how much money it would take for Swansea Town to let him go. One reporter wondered whether Ford would be amused at the prospect of either Ivor or Ray Daniel taking his place as the most expensive player in history. All the talk was of these three players, all, of course, Swansea-born. Daniel had been selected straight from the Arsenal reserve side and in the game stole the limelight from his senior team-mate in the English eleven, Leslie Compton.

With Allchurch at number 10, Wales now ran into a little form, beating Northern Ireland, Portugal and Switzerland. All was set for what was to be the memorable 1951-2 season, one in which Wales allowed its Football Association to celebrate its 75th Anniversary by sharing the Home International Championship with England, something which had last happened in the triple-tie with Scotland in 1938-9.

Since Wales had not won the Championship outright since 1936-7, there was a general concurrence that Wales were the real winners in this their anniversary season. Ivor certainly enjoyed the festivities to the full. The season started with a noisy, excited, capacity crowd at Ninian Park to see a Welsh team, including several youngsters, take on England who were fielding such stars as Alf Ramsey, Billy Wright, Ton Finney, and Nat Lofthouse. The game started sensationally when after three minutes the Welsh winger Billy Foulkes scored with his first kick in international football. Eddie Baily equalised nine minutes later and that was the end of the scoring. What followed was a poor but thrilling encounter in which the 'moral victory' went to Wales, who, with a little more luck, could have gained their first victory over England since 1938. Ford, perhaps, should have scored the winner, although he had a tireless game and gave centre-half Barrass a real buffeting. The highlight of the afternoon, as was so often the case, was the battle between Sherwood and Finney, but what was heartening was the form of the Welsh youngsters; Daniel in defence, Foulkes and Clarke on the wings and Allchurch at inside-forward. Initially Ivor had been ordered to lie deep, leaving only four forward 'in the Brazilian style', but he was seen to far greater effect in the second half when he joined the front four. In spite of the attentions of Billy Wright, he was thought to have had a useful if unobtrusive match.

A month later came one of the highlights of the soccer calendar, the visit of Wales to Glasgow's Hampden Park, the largest and most intimidating stadium in the British Isles. Scotland were regarded, even more than England, as a soccer nation, and if anything there was even greater respect for the skills of its great masters of the football craft, as well as the strength of its great defenders. There were certainly outstanding names in the Scotland line-up that day, but they did not play well. Tommy Orr took a penalty but could only hit the post, Willie Waddell was bottled up by Sherwood, and the much vaunted Billy Steel could do little against Roy Paul, who seven years later described him as the best British inside-left. At centre-half was the great Willie Woodburn, but he was nowhere to be seen when, in the last minute of the game with the stadium already emptying, Roy Clarke centred from the

*The Welsh team that beat the United Kingdom 3-2 in the 75th anniversary match of the F.A. of Wales at Ninian Park, 1951.*
*Back row: R. Paul, R. Daniel, W. Shortt, R. Burgess, A. Sherwood, I. Allchurch.*
*Front row: W. Foulkes, W. Morris, W. Barnes, T. Ford, R. Clarke.*

left for Allchurch to nod the ball at speed past Cowan in goal. 'A perfect goal – a real match-winner – from the man with the curly golden hair' was how one report summed up the moment which ruined the afternoon for a huge crowd of Scots.

The Championship was clinched four months later at the Vetch Field, Swansea, where Wales were playing for the first time since 1928. The venue was thought appropriate given the presence of four players with Swansea connections, but it was a poor game played in difficult conditions, with Ivor scoring the most satisfactory of the goals in a 3-0 victory. In many ways the real highlight of the anniversary season had come earlier in December when, in a special commemorative game, Wales played The Rest of the United Kingdom at Ninian Park and beat them 3-2. This was one of those occasions which, as is often the case when there is nothing at stake, could have been a real flop. There was a disappointing crowd of about 35,000 as compared to the 60,000 who had turned up six weeks earlier to see England; there were few rosettes and rattles in evidence; there was little singing from a largely silent crowd. To cap it all, there was a blustery wind.

However, notwithstanding these auguries, the game took off. Wales, of course, were determined to impress, and for an hour they played fast skilful football which 'had the crack U.K. defence staggering'. As early as the second minute a brilliant run by Burgess allowed Allchurch to head a goal past his now familiar adversaries Cowan and Wright. Later goals came from Ford and again Allchurch. With about 25 minutes to go, Wales were coasting home 3-0 against eleven men who had obviously never recovered from being asked to play in white shirts, blue satin shorts and green socks. For all the class of Young and Wright in defence and the Scottish artistry of Gordon Smith and Fleming in attack, this assortment of talented individuals could not compete with the well-established rhythms of Wales. But, as one reporter commented, 'Someone always spoils a party', and on this afternoon that someone was a Charlie 'Cannonball' Fleming, an uncapped player from East Fife who fired a shot from thirty yards that was as powerful as any ever seen by Walley Barnes. Thereafter, the birthday boys had a game on their hands as the U.K. suddenly jelled. Les Medley conjured up a goal, and Wales were forced to defend their lead robustly. During this period, Burgess and Barnes were thought to have had their finest games for Wales, and Sherwood was as solid as ever. But all that determined defence at the end did not eclipse the earlier impression of a Wales 'on song', with Ford and Allchurch the real stars. Above all, Ivor's performance had been convincing; for Clifford Webb, 'Allchurch was the wizard in all this Welsh revelry – he might have scored four.' He was, of course, still only twenty-one.

Clearly, this was a good Welsh team. Indeed, Clifford Webb thought it the best Welsh team for twenty years. Wally Barnes of Arsenal, proud to have been its captain, boasted that it was 'the finest team ever to have represented our country'. With the pride came a good deal of analysis, but Barnes was absolutely right in his emphasis. As Roy Paul and others pointed out, on every Welsh shirt was the motto *'Gorau chwarae cyd-chwarae'*, 'Team play is the best play'; that was very much the point. Every player spoke of their pride in putting on the red shirt, and there was a feeling that national honour was there to be defended. There was every incentive for Welsh players to see how good they were in the company of the English and Scottish household names. Resources, however, were limited; there were disputed selections, tending often to concern Cardiff City players, but for the most part the team tended to pick itself. This then was more like a club side; there was really no point, as Roy Paul explained, in players going for a flashy individual performance at the expense of team play. Tactics were the key, and they would be worked out amongst the players themselves. The plan would come from senior players like Barnes and Burgess with officials, the trainer, and even the Medical Officer, Doc. Hughes, chipping in. The hallmark was, as Barnes explained, intelligence combined with national fervour. The contrast was with England, who often seemed to be a team in turmoil in these years. To an extent, of course, the English suffered from an embarrassment of riches; there were constant team changes, with the inevitable outcome that individuals played for themselves. Furthermore, as Roy Paul pointed out, in the recent past players who put on the English shirt tended to become too defensive.

That 1951-2 season gave the Welsh team a new dignity. It was apparent in their very appearance, for unveiled at the U.K. game was a new strip in which the famous imperial and somewhat incandescent red shirt was graced with a huge coat or arms, with dragon and motto resplendent. No team in the world looked so good, so official, and as they ran out those of us on the terraces knew that just as they would die for Wales, so we would die for them. That dignity and sense of identity were to be needed for in the aftermath of the 1952 Champ-

*'The Duke meets Ivor' . . . England v. Wales (Wembley), 1952.*

ionship there was a nemesis; Wales were to win only one of their next twelve games. During that period, it was proving difficult to beat strong England and Scotland sides, and some heavy defeats were experienced on European soil. In these circumstances, once again, comfort had to be taken from individual performances.

In November 1952, Wales played at Wembley for the first time. English fans were warned to look out for Allchurch, who was described by Bob Ferrier as 'the complete, natural, intuitive inside-forward – the Mozart of football'. For their part the Welsh players were warned about the spongy turf which eight of them were experiencing for the first time in their careers. Ivor was thrilled by the splendour and grandeur of Wembley, and by the pulsating cheers; it was all more impressive than Hampden Park. However, the stadium also served to inspire England; a team described by Ivor as 'great', and 'inspired' and who played 'truly artistic football' in spite of the loss of centre-half Froggatt. England won, 5-2, and Wales were shocked by the drubbing they received, which disappointed not only them but also the thousands of their fans who had travelled to London. Welsh consolation came from two Ford goals, one of which was the best of the match.

Allchurch's performance for the Welsh League team in Belfast in 1951 had prompted the reporter Gwilym Evans to ask whether there was 'a better inside-forward in Britain?' In terms of domestic football, it was already generally accepted that Ivor was one of the best players outside the First Division. At international level there was always an expectation that he would make a telling contribution. When Wales went to Belfast in April 1953, John Charles who had first played for Wales before Allchurch (in 1950) but who was only now being released to play regularly for his country, scored twice, but once again it was Ivor who caught the eye and was identified by many as the man of the match. For John Graydon, 'Mr Magic revealed his "radar-like accuracy"', his uncanny positional sense, and his ability to glide into scoring positions.' Ivor, Graydon suggested, was putting colour back into British football where there had been a decline in the level of inside-forward play since the days of Alex James and Charles Buchan. In the previous six years, he thought Ademir of Brazil the greatest inside-forward in the world, but Allchurch was in the top six.

A month later, the sheer pace of France condemned Wales to a 6-1 defeat in Paris, but Ivor scored the game's opening goal, and more than one account referred to his brilliance. In November 1953, Wales forced a draw at Hampden in front of 71,000 people, after having been 3-1 down with twenty minutes to go. In part the turning point had been Ivor's switching from too-defensive a position which he had adopted in the first half. Thereafter he 'foraged' more effectively and scored a memorable goal which rather eclipsed John Charles's two strikes. Apparently, Ivor had 'weaved through from some distance' before 'unleashing a tremendous shot from well outside the penalty area', which gave goalkeeper Farm no chance.

In the early 1950's the Home Championship was still the absolutely vital competition for Wales; it was still the only route to the World Cup for United Kingdom teams. Europe, however, was a growing reality, and Wales clearly needed to establish its credentials in that arena. In an increasing number of matches played on the Continent, there was little success, although Wales had never actually lost to a foreign side at home. That of course had been England's proud boast until that famous day in November 1953 when the Hungarians had won 6-3 at Wembley. The Welsh record went in September 1954, when the Yugoslavs were victorious, 3-1, at Ninian Park. The lesson learnt by Wales was perhaps not quite as salutary as that handed out to England but the circumstances were even more dramatic, and in the process something was learnt about European methods. 'Weep for Wales', said Bob Pennington, for this match should have been easily won. It was lost because, with European rules applying, a substitute came on to replace an apparently uninjured player and then proceeded to score a hat-trick with his only three shots of the game. Wales had deserved better, for they had matched the Yugoslavs in every respect. Derek Tapscott had impressed in what was only his second game, but there was no doubt that, once again, Allchurch was the star. This was an 'outstanding' performance by a player to whom the press were attaching a £50,000 tag. Again he rewarded the 50,000 crowd with a memorable goal: after a 50 yard burst he took a pass from Paul, beat several defenders and scored off the post from an 'impossible angle' at a time when winger Billy Reed lay concussed in the goalmouth. This

*Austria – Vienna 1954 . . . 'eyes on the ball'.*

goal had given Wales a 52 minute lead and it was only a world-class performance by goalkeeper Vladimir Beara which denied Ivor another three.

Compared with the 1952 championship side, there were two significant changes in the Welsh line-up for that match. In goal the reliable, jovial and aptly named Shortt had been replaced by Arsenal's Jack Kelsey, a player of real class, who was a timely addition to a defence that was in the process of losing Barnes and Burgess, its two great post-war stalwarts. Meanwhile John Charles, whose unique talents had been obvious since his 1950 début, was now regularly available for Wales to select either in defence or attack.

These two Swansea-born players had totally redefined what later observers would describe as the spine of the Welsh team. They had both played in the Yugoslav defeat and in the match narrowly lost to Scotland in 1954. As yet however they had not appeared in a game against England, although Charles had already made some individual impact in that annual fixture which was always regarded as the greatest and most significant challenge. His first game against England was in Cardiff in 1953, one of those defeats that haunt Welsh memories. Wales played brilliantly that day and lost 4-1. For Roy Paul, that was the day when the giant Welshman became 'King Charles'; the image that Paul, and all of us who were there, took away from that game was the sight of Charles leaping above Harry Johnston, Gil Merrick and indeed the bar to head for goal. What Charles himself remembered from that day was 'a brilliant shot by Allchurch' which had given Wales the lead. In 1954 Charles played his first game at Wembley where once again Wales took the lead, temporarily lost players through injury, and then lost the game. The final score was 3-2 with Charles scoring both Welsh goals.

At last, in 1955, Wales took on England with all the star players in position. Most of those men were Swansea-born: Kelsey in goal, John and Mel Charles in the half-back line and Ford, Allchurch and Cliff Jones up front; meanwhile at right half was Roy Paul who learned his skills at the Vetch. The line-up that day comes readily to mind because, for the first time since 1938, Wales beat England. Alf Sherwood who had first played against England in 1946, was the proud captain in a game in which his defence had to withstand the challenge of both Matthews and Finney, the two greatest wingers of the post-war era, as well as the threat of Nat Lofthouse and Don Revie. On the day Sher-

*Wales v. Scotland, 1955.*
*Back row: Mel Charles, Stuart Williams, Jack Kelsey, John Charles, Roy Paul, Ivor.*
*Front row: Derek Tapscott, Noel Kinsey, Alf Sherwood, Trevor Ford, Cliff Jones.*

wood was magnificent, as were so many of the Welsh side. Trevor Ford had another ding-dong battle with Billy Wright, but the two Welsh goals came from Derek Tapscott and Cliff Jones, who, in the opinion of some, looked a better winger than the two English greats. At centre-half John Charles blotted-out Lofthouse, although he did suffer the indignity of unavoidably heading an own goal. As Wales held on to their lead, Allchurch's role became crucial, for with Paul limping on the wing, he had to drop back to left half. A grateful Paul thought that this was Ivor's 'finest ever game for Wales'.

All the subsequent memoirs of the players involved reveal how much 22 October 1955 meant to the eleven Welshman who earned victory on that day. The memory became all the sweeter since it was to be five years before another Home championship game was won. These were not always enjoyable times, and Welsh players had to endure all kinds of mixed emotions. For example 20 April 1955 had been a very enjoyable and memorable day in its own way. In Belfast, Northern Ireland had played the better football but lost 3-2 as a result of an 'opportunistic' John Charles hat-trick. But what had given most pleasure that day was the fact that Len Allchurch won his first cap. For the first time in 72 years there were two sets of brothers in the Welsh team, Swansea boys all. Len, of course, was not only a brother, but also, like Mel Charles, a Swansea team-mate. One can well imagine the pleasure which Ivor took in seeing Swansea Town honoured in this way. Furthermore, it is easy to forget what Allchurch had been going through, playing week-in-week-out for unfashionable Swansea, and then turning up at Ninian Park, Hampden Park and Wembley for internationals, where great things were now expected from him. In that regular transition, which he had to make six or seven times a year, the Swansea dimension can only have helped. Wingers of course were crucially important in Ivor's game plan; he specialised in defence-splitting passes to them, and he was always looking for the return as he burst forward. In the mid-1950's brother Len, Cliff Jones and Terry Medwin were all Swansea wingers whom Ivor took into the national team. Very soon Jones and Medwin were caught up in the emergence of a great side at Tottenham.

After 1955 things turned a little sour for Wales as they did for Ivor Allchurch personally. Jack Kelsey was to comment in his memoirs how silent he found Ivor on match days; clearly he was not at ease with the Swansea man, who would remain in a corner and only speak when spoken to. Writing in 1957, Kelsey's judgement was that he 'had not seen Ivor play for Wales as I know he can for Swansea.' This view, somewhat surprising in the light of many of the earlier assessments that had been made by knowledgeable observers, came at a time when Allchurch was temporarily out of the national side. After a run of twenty seven caps, he began to experience a period of ankle and thigh injuries which led to what Jim Hill referred to as a period of 'despair'. At the time, Ivor's place in the Welsh side went to the slight, dark, intense and classy Roy Vernon of Blackburn Rovers who was to have a run of seven games in the number 10 shirt which had belonged to Ivor for seven very eventful years.

Vernon found himself in the Welsh side that was facing an unprecedented challenge. For the first time, the United Kingdom nations would have to qualify for the 1958 World Cup Finals in open competition rather than through the Home International Championship. England's virtually guaranteed hold had been broken, but now the other three nations were faced with a realistic assessment of their European Standing. Wales without Allchurch had to cope with the might of East Germany, and Czechoslovakia. In the event the Welsh won both home games, but lost in Leipzig and Prague. They had failed to qualify, but had come second to Czechoslovakia; that, it transpired, gave them a second chance.

In another group, Egypt withdrew rather than face Israel, at which point F.I.F.A. ruled that Israel would have to play in a qualifying match against a country drawn by lots from amongst the seven runners-up in the other groups. Wales won that draw, and so had only two games against Israel between them and the World Cup Finals in Sweden. From the first game in Tel Aviv in January 1958 Ivor Allchurch was fit and available and was recalled. The second chapter of his remarkable career was about to open. Once again he was a 'Man of Wales', the number 10 shirt was back where it belonged.

# CHAPTER FOUR

# The Sykes Academy

## 1952-3

In September 1952, Ivor and Esme became officially engaged. For them, it had been a long two years keeping their betrothal secret, but, now, they could tell the world! When the engagement was announced, by the nature of such things in those days, Ivor was deemed to have 'settled down'. Many people were delighted with the news; none more so than the supporters of Swansea Town. They read into the tea leaves that, because Esme was a Swansea girl, this arrangement would help to keep Ivor at the Vetch Field. Actually, the converse could have been true. Once married, if a move meant that Ivor's career would be furthered, the young couple might have been prepared to leave the town.

At the Vetch Field there were few new faces to excite the supporters as the new season approached. Indeed, the only senior newcomer was Gwyn Groves, a goal-keeper who had been signed as cover for Johnny King, who had been 'called up'. There was, though, a significant youth arrival – John Charles's brother, Mel had been signed before any predators appeared.

In explaining the lack of acquisitions, the Swansea chairman resorted to the policy which he had outlined during the previous campaign. He announced, 'We intend to develop local talent to the exclusion of other than minimal purchases.' It was not what the Swansea supporters wanted to hear. Nevertheless, over twenty-four thousand people were at the Vetch Field for the opening match of the 1952-3 season when Sheffield United were the visitors. That crowd saw Ivor score for the Swans, but the' Blades' take both points. After five matches, two of which had been won and one drawn, the Swans found themselves in mid-table.

Despite the mediocre start, at the time, Ivor felt that there was the basis of a good side at the Vetch. He believed that if they continued to score goals, whilst tightening their defence they would begin to climb

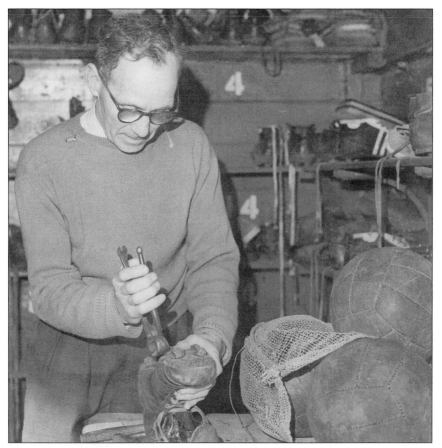

*Head of the Academy . . . Mr. (Joe) Sykes in the boot room.*

the league table. There were, also, the youngsters to savour; players of the calibre of Terry Medwin, Harry Griffiths, Cliff Jones, and Ivor's brother, Len. Later, these players were to be joined by the 17 year-old Mel Charles, who, during the season, was to appear in twenty, first team matches. For their part, Medwin and Griffiths each played in all but two of the matches in that campaign, and in the process, both added to the store of their experience.

In retrospect, it is interesting to observe the side which was later to have such a remarkable impact upon the Second Division beginning to take shape. Even though such a development was not as evident at the time, the youngsters who were included made a more than useful contribution to the improved form of the team. So much so, indeed, that when the season ended the Swans found themselves eleventh place in their division, eleven places higher than had been the case at the end of the previous campaign.

As far as the Swansea directors were concerned, this outcome appeared as to justify the policy which they had formulated. Indeed, the side which drew 1-1 with Fulham in the November of that season, comprised ten Welshmen, eight of whom were Swansea-born. Ivor enthused about this development. Team spirit, he reported in his column in the local paper, was 'tremendous', with the 'Swansea boys feeling that, as when they had played for the schoolboys, they were representing their town.' Terry Medwin remembering those days forty years later, agreed, but made the point that 'At that time, we all looked up to Ivor. He was "the greatest" as far as we were concerned.'

At the time, too, the *Sunday Express* held the same opinion as Medwin and his colleagues. Prior to the start of the 1952-3 season, they published an article under the title: 'Ivor – the idol of Wales'. In it they summed up the young man's skills as they saw them. 'Allchurch has something of the body-swerve of David Jack, the shooting venom of Billy Walker, and the defence-splitting pass of Alex James'. Not content with that, they bracketed the Swansea man with Billy Meredith, Dixie Dean, and Stanley Matthews, and stated: 'Of all the players who captured the headlines last season, there was one with the hallmark of greatness – Ivor Allchurch.'

In spite of being flattered by these comments, as the *Sunday Express* article went on to show, Ivor still had in mind the criticism which had been made of him during earlier seasons. His response was to work hard in order to remedy whatever shortcomings he was conscious of having. The Swansea trainer, Frank Barson, put this into context when, having likened Ivor, again, to Billy Walker, said: 'Ivor is a professional. He trains hard and, if he doesn't come up to his own standards in practice games he returns, alone, to the ground for more practice.' Late in September 1952, Arsenal offered £30,000 for the Swansea man, but, again, the offer was rejected. The press interpreted the Swansea reaction simply as a negotiating ploy. Several papers forecast that the record fee at the time (£35,000 which had been paid for Jackie Sewell) would be surpassed when Allchurch left Swansea. In reply to this, the

*Superstitious Ivor?*

Swansea chairman issued a statement which, he claimed, reflected the annoyance of the board. 'How many more times do we have to say that Allchurch is NOT for sale?' No one from the press responded.

The local paper, no doubt, wishing to ensure that that continued to be true, emphasised that 'The Swans are not a one man team'. Even though no one pretended that Ivor was not the key player in the

Swansea side, the paper had a point. When the season drew to a close, the leading goal-scorers in the side were all graduates of the Sykes academy. Terry Medwin scored sixteen times, Ivor was second with fifteen, whilst Harry Griffiths scored ten. Between them the three players had scored more than half the goals registered by the team. They were a formidable strike force which played with style.

The *pièce de résistance* of Ivor's season had been a first half 'hat-trick' against Brentford in an Easter fixture at the Vetch. Each of the goals was indicative of a different aspect of the Allchurch armoury of skills. The first was a well-executed header, glancing the ball beyond the reach of a diving goalkeeper. The second demonstrated the power of his shooting plus his awareness in the area. In this instance, having beaten two men, Ivor found himself facing four other Brentford defenders, massed in front of their goalkeeper. His response was to hit a rasping drive which hit full back, Munro, in the midriff, so hard, that he collapsed on the goal line. As the ball rebounded off the unfortunate defender, Allchurch 'crashed it into the net'. Afterwards, the Brentford back needed attention for several minutes. The final goal of the three illustrated Ivor's mesmerising ball-control, pace and determination. Receiving the ball just inside the Brentford half, he avoided two tackles and strode through the middle. The visiting centre half slipped, and Allchurch skipped around him and between the two full backs both of whom were coming to tackle him. Then he was confronted by the goalkeeper who had raced out to narrow his angle. Ivor took the ball to the right of the 'keeper, who then dived at his feet, knocking the Swansea man over, though, not before he had directed the ball into the unguarded net. The Swansea crowd rose to their hero. It was his first 'hat-trick' for the club, and, as someone said at the time, a Trevor Ford would have been proud of each of the goals.

Three weeks earlier, Ivor had performed the role of provider in a comprehensive 4-1 victory at St. Andrews. *The People* in it's report of the match enthused about how 'The ball control of Ivor Allchurch constantly had the Birmingham defence going the wrong way'. The *Sunday Express* version read 'Birmingham could not hold Ivor Allchurch the Welsh inside left wizard with the mesmerising feet', and 'Allchurch was at his irresistible best and could not be quietened'.

With Medwin at centre-forward, Griffiths at outside-right, and Cliff Jones's brother, Brin, at inside-right, that part of the season was exciting for the Swansea fans and players alike. Indeed, during the period around Easter, the Swans scored fifteen goals and conceded just three. At the time, all at the Vetch felt that everything was falling into place. Joe Sykes was revelling in it all. His boys were 'coming through' with a vengeance.

Nonetheless, there were, still, those who argued that Ivor should get away from Swansea and join a first-division club. David Jack, writing of a visit to Swansea where he had seen the Swans training on the beach, was one of them. He reminded his readers that Ted Drake, the Chelsea manager, had made a record bid during the previous week for the Swansea number ten. 'That', he wrote, 'was one of the dozens of offers which have been made for this 23-year-old, shy, unspoiled football genius.' Then, answering his own question – 'Is it a good thing that Allchurch remains with Swansea?' he wrote:

> 'Two years ago Ivor Allchurch was the most promising youngster in football. He still is just that, and until he joins a good First Division side his promise will never be fulfilled,' Jack quoted a First Division manager, who was of the opinion that: 'Ivor Allchurch is being wasted in the Second Division . . . The longer he plays with second-division players, the more like them he will become. In his own interests he should get into top-class football as quickly as possible.'

Ivor, so Jack reported, disagreed. He told him that, 'From international experience I have discovered that there is less crowding and more room to . . . play top class soccer. I'd say that it is harder to do so in this division.' The Swansea manager, Billy McCandless, no doubt wishing to retain his star player, pointed out to Jack that, 'He is on the League's maximum wage and, already, he's been paid one benefit with another due before he is twenty-seven.' Nonetheless, in the face of persistent 'sniping' from those who believed that Ivor should be playing in Division One, it appeared that the wagons were circling at the Vetch. Whatever happened, it seemed that the Vetch authorities wished to keep Ivor. The club's supporters were of the same mind. Yet, at this distance an objective view would suggest that David Jack and others who argued that Ivor should be playing in a better class of football, were probably right. Certainly those who left Swansea for the First Division, such as Cliff Jones, have no doubt that Ivor should have gone, and that he would have been an even greater player had he done so.

Almost forty years later, Cliff Jones and Terry Medwin, still spoke in awed tones about their former team-mate. 'There was nobody like him!' Medwin said, 'He had so many skills which all the coaching in the world could not reproduce. He glided past people as if they weren't there. He had balance and grace which I have never seen since. And his shooting! He'd hit them from thirty or forty yards like rockets.' Cliff Jones, who played with Terry at Tottenham and for Wales, agreed. 'Ivor was an incredible player. He had such great control, deceptive pace and a tremendous temperament. I feel very privileged to have known and played with Ivor – a graceful, stylish person both on and off the field.' Each of these tributes ended on an almost apologetic note, 'but he should have gone to a first-division side.' And they spoke those words as if they went beyond their right in criticising the man they both revered.

Leaving all that aside, despite Bill Shankly's famous statement, there is more to life than football. In Ivor's case the most important event of 1953 was his marriage to Esme. The couple tied the knot in the June of that year and settled in the Mumbles district of Swansea. Ivor still lived for football, but, now, the newlyweds could think about establishing their own dynasty. Both of them wanted a large family.

## 1953-4

When the players returned to the Vetch for pre-season training, Ivor found that he had acquired a 'batman'. Young Mel Nurse, who joined the Swansea ground staff that summer, attached himself to Ivor and would fetch and carry for his 'officer' as required. Ivor, Mel recalls, was his idol, and just to be in his company was sufficient reward for the boy. Interestingly, this arrangement continued even when both men were members of the Swansea first team and even when they were internationals. And according to Mel, forty years later, there were dozens of boys who would have jumped at the chance of filling his shoes. Such was the appeal of Ivor John Allchurch.

That season, though, Ivor's satisfaction with his status as a newly married man was not matched by success at the Vetch. After the relative euphoria of the last quarter of the previous season, most commentators expected the Swans to be successful in the 1953-4 campaign. Unfortunately the converse was true. Inexplicably, by the end of 1953, the team had gained only twenty points: whilst, in the second half of the season they were even less effective. Ultimately, the team finished just one place above Brentford, who were relegated.

At the time the Swansea critics were out in force, blaming the Board for not being willing to strengthen the side. The directors, however, ignored these arguments and, on the grounds that they believed the club had too many players, allowed several, more than useful performers to leave. Among those was former captain Billy Lucas. On top of that, Frank Barson resigned because of ill health and Manager McCandless was 'carpeted' for not involving himself to a sufficient degree in training the players. It was clear that the Swansea board did not hold with the business maxim that it is necessary to speculate to accumulate. As far as they were concerned, the club's needs would have to be met from the incredible conveyor belt to be found in Swansea Schools' football.


*1954-5*


Meantime, from a personal point of view, Ivor could look back on another productive season. He had gained a further four international 'caps', had finished the season as leading scorer with seventeen goals, and had scored a second 'hat-trick', against Fulham. But it was a decision taken by the board in June 1954 which gave him the greatest comfort. After advertising for a player-coach, they appointed Ronnie Burgess, the Welsh International wing-half. Although Burgess was, then, thirty-seven years of age, he had been an outstanding player for Tottenham and for Wales and was a man of vast experience. He came to Swansea with glowing references both as a player and a leader of men, and it was generally held that his presence would make all the difference to the performances of the Swansea side.

His first match in Swansea colours appeared to confirm those expectations, although it was Ivor, again, who attracted the headlines on the following day. For some reason, Swansea's opening game of the 1954-5 season started fifteen minutes before the remainder of the Football League matches which were played that day. The visitors were West Ham United, old footballing adversaries of the Swans. They had a fine team at the time and included players like John Bond, Noel Cantwell, Malcolm Allison and Dave Sexton in their line up. With

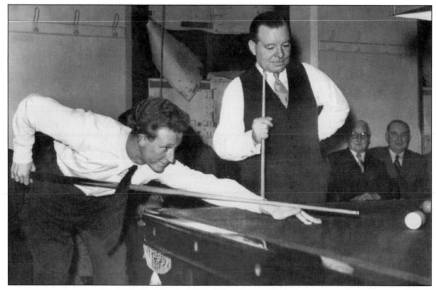

*Joe Davis admires the Allchurch style.*

such opposition and Ronnie Burgess in the home team along with eight Swansea-born players, the Vetch Field that day was agog with expectation.

Despite the presence of Burgess, Ivor Allchurch retained the captaincy and led his side out to a thunderous reception from a crowd of twenty-five thousand. Among those who observed this fact from the press box was Percy Young, who later, in his book *Football Year* recalled what happened in the early minutes of the match:

> 'Within three minutes of the whistle there was a goal. It was Allchurch's goal . . . The papers were correct. Allchurch was the finest inside-forward in the game . . . It had been this way. Allchurch, receiving the ball just beyond the half-way line, veered north-eastward, feinting the while. Ten yards from the corner flag the position was without hope. A posse of defenders harassed, and to contrive a neat, carefully pointed pass, appeared as impossible as to outwit, single-footed, so many claret-coloured men . . . Suddenly the fight foot swung. The ball lifted and, windswept, went directly into the distant net.'

That day, as the Swansea supporters streamed away from the ground at the end of the match, they did so with high expectations. Burgess, Allchurch and the young Turks playing such sparkling football would surely, sweep all before them! Had they been asked, West Ham would have agreed with them. John Bond did. Many years later, reflecting upon their defeat by five goals to two, he said: 'We didn't know what hit us. Swansea were brilliant that day and Allchurch was outstanding at the centre of their brilliance.' That day, Ivor chalked up yet another record as a result of his genius. He scored the first goal in the English League for the 1954-5 season.

Given not only the extent of the victory but its quality, following the game, both Ivor and Ronnie Burgess were ebullient. Burgess expressed himself delighted with the football played by the young side (at 24, Ivor was the 'old man' of the forward-line). He thought that they would do well in the season ahead and, 'If they continue playing like that, they'll take some stopping'. Ivor, whose sobriquet, 'The Golden Boy', had become established to the exclusion of many others coined by journalists, agreed. Would all the talk of his having to leave Swansea for first-division football now be put to rest? Only time would tell.

Meantime, rival managers, seeing Ivor as the key man in the Swansea forward line set out to stifle his creativity. For example, later in the season, Ted Fenton, the West Ham manager, anxious to avoid another drubbing at the hands of the Swansea side, took two players to Wembley with him to watch Allchurch playing for Wales. The objective, he said at the time, was to find a way to keep Allchurch out of the game. Others, distinctly less scientific in their methods, tried to achieve the same end by, 'The brutality of their tackling', as one writer put it. This was an all-too-common approach, and another journalist was 'amazed that Ivor had escaped serious injury as a result of some of the tackling to which he is subjected'. Clearly, Ivor's experiences as a sixteen-year-old in the Welsh League were standing him in good stead.

Unfortunately, though, the euphoria enjoyed following the opening match at the Vetch Field evaporated, first in Yorkshire and then in Lancashire, as Doncaster and Blackburn beat the Swans in their initial away matches. And later, whilst the team was successful when it played at home (it was unbeaten at the Vetch until January) its away form left much to be desired. One result of this was that, at the end of what can only be described as a colourful season, the side had scored 86 goals but had conceded only three less. There were some remarkable wins but, equally as many striking defeats. The Swans beat Ipswich 6-1, and Port Vale 7-1, but lost 0-7 to Bristol Rovers and 1-5 to Fulham. Nevertheless, the football was always exciting, and the final position of the club in the second-division – tenth – was a considerable improvement on the previous term.

It was obvious to everyone that there was little wrong with the attack. Goals were scored from many parts of the pitch, most of them by Swansea born players, all of whom were internationals. Ivor led the pack with 20 goals, Harry Griffiths was second with 16, while Mel Charles scored 13, Terry Medwin 12, Cliff Jones 10 and Len Allchurch 7. The Joe Sykes academy of starlets was beginning to create an unforgettable impression.

For his part, during the campaign, Ivor played some magnificent matches, reaching the pinnacle of his season with the game against Ipswich. The *Empire News* report of that game put this performance in a nutshell; 'Allchurch cracked in three of Swansea's goals and orchestrated the rest'. The *People* reported 'Three Allchurch rockets left defenders bewildered', and the *Sunday Express* reporter, who must have taken a measuring tape with him, wrote 'The Golden Boy scored three spectacular goals from 25, 35, and 45 yards. This star', he added, 'has no peer'.

Meanwhile, throughout the season, the press were always alert to the possibility of an Allchurch-for-transfer story. Ivor, however, seemed to float over the flood of enquiries from these journalists with a new buoyancy. Following the opening day victory over West Ham, he told reporters; 'Now that we have Ronnie Burgess, an international of vast experience, to play with us and coach us, we should do well'. Then, in December, he set out to reassure Swansea Town supporters yet again. In his own column in the *South Wales Evening Post* he wrote:

'I would like to say to the people of Swansea, I am one of you. I am happy with you, and as long as I am happy, I am staying with you!'

At that, one wag on Swansea's 'Tanner Bank' announced in a fruity, clerical voice, 'And behold, the multitude were placated. The favourite son was to stay in his father's house.'

Notwithstanding their chameleon-like league form, the team had done well in the F.A. Cup. Blackburn Rovers, who had beaten the Swans twice in the league, were defeated at Ewood Park, and, at the end of January, Stoke City came to the Vetch Field. Stoke had also 'done the double' over the Swans were quote as firm favourites to win the tie. In front of 27,892 people, a new record for the Vetch Field, the men in white confounded the odds by winning by three goals to one. A Cardiff-based journalist, 'Citizen', after crediting Ivor with being' The Star of the match', put the kind of football played by Swansea Town at the time into perspective, when he wrote: 'The "clicking" of the attack saw the whole team play with a new zeal as if embarked on a Jihad or holy war,' and 'But one wonders what would have happened had the Swans been up against a more talented forward line.' Despite that caveat, the journalist expressed the opinion that 'If the Swans are drawn at home . . . then their chances of survival must be rated as rosy.'

Consequently, even when the club's opponents in the last sixteen of the competition proved to be mighty Sunderland (the 'Bank of England' team of the period) there was confidence abroad at the Vetch. Yet, even before the match which caught the imagination of the football world in general, Ivor was, still, being dogged with the 'Are you leaving Swansea?' question. The player's response was to emphasise the positive aspects of life at the Vetch. All the same, there was a note of reservation in what he had to say:

> 'This is the best Swansea team I have played in. We have a fair chance of promotion, and if we miss out, we must stand a better chance next season . . . I shall do my utmost to help them get promotion . . . but if my club does not reach the First Division within, say, the next season or two, I shall reconsider my position.'

The drama which was to unfold within eighteen months of Allchurch having voiced these sentiments was to lead to just such a reconsideration, and to result in a sad outcome for Swansea Town supporters.

Meantime, another record F.A. Cup 'gate' greeted Sunderland and the Swans at the Vetch on that February day in 1955. The high-priced players in the Sunderland side – like Shackleton, Hedley, Bingham and Chisholm – were, clearly, an attraction, yet, so was that vivacious Swansea side. And, to the delight of the home supporters, their favourites more than held their own. Indeed, most commentators felt that the 2-2 draw which ensued rather flattered the 'Wearsiders'. As far as Ivor's contribution was concerned, the press, comparing his performance with that of Len Shackleton, came to the collective conclusion that honours were even. In the replay, however, Ivor was given the greater credit, but, unfortunately, Sunderland won the tie by the only goal of the game.

The balm which soothed the Swansea fans' disappointment at this defeat, was the fact that their men had shown that they could compete on level terms with one of the best sides in the First Division. After the replay, Manager McCandless, Ronnie Burgess and skipper, Ivor Allchurch expressed their agreement with this view, as did the Sunderland camp. These comments were music to the ears of the Swansea supporters, and McCandless, waxing eloquent said that the team was 'beginning to gel. Wine takes time to mature, so do football teams.'

### 1955-6

With so much promise having been shown during the previous campaign, during the prelude to the 1955-6 season, the management and staff at the Vetch were in confident mood. Ivor, who was captain again, believed that the club had what was necessary to win promotion to Division One. He was of the opinion that there was so much talent in, what would today be termed 'the squad', that, barring injuries they 'ought to do it'. The supporters, certainly wanted to believe that such an outcome was possible, but, at the Vetch there was always that 'sneaky feeling' that something would go wrong.

Within days of the players returning for pre-season training, it did: manager, Billy McCandless died. Although McCandless had had his critics on the Swansea board during the previous season, this was a blow to the club. Whatever his short-comings may have been, he was a very experienced manager, and there was no one else at the Vetch possessing such advantage. Given what was to happen in the season ahead, it is possible that, had he lived, McCandless might have been able to persuade the Swansea board to change their minds at a crucial stage in the campaign.

It was this board which, on the death of McCandless, decided that they would not replace him 'for the time being', Instead, they gave

Ronnie Burgess the title 'Team Manager', and established a three-man selection committee, with Joe Sykes and Ivor joining him for that purpose. That decision was innovative from the playing point of view, but one problem with it was that the trio acted as a *de facto* management team. In so doing, they had to liaise with the Swansea board, yet none of them had any experience of this role. Despite their fame as footballers, their background lent itself to a tendency to be deferential as far as businessmen were concerned. Balance sheets and the like were not part of their language nor of their understanding. Since it was the influence of ultra-cautious business decisions which was to result in the club failing in its challenge for promotion just when the prize appeared to be within its grasp, that weakness can be seen to have been crucial.

The first five games of the 1955-6 season gave the pessimists among Swansea supporters more stimulus than the optimists. Whilst both home matches were won, the three played on opponents' grounds were lost. It was hardly the start which had been hoped for. Ivor and his management colleagues expressed themselves 'disappointed', but felt that things would improve. Before that happened, however Esme and Ivor were devastated when the second baby which Esme had been carrying was still-born. Losing a child at such a stage is a traumatic experience for any couple, but, unlike men in many trades and professions, Ivor couldn't blend quietly into the background of life to comfort Esme and deal with his own grief. He had to carry on in his very public role. The show, as it were, had to go on. With the team not having achieved what many felt was its potential, this was a difficult period for Ivor, and he and Esme were glad to have their families around to support them. Sadly, the young couple were to lose two other babies in similar circumstances. As often happens, they both felt that the despair of these traumatic experiences helped to draw them even closer together.

In those September days in 1955 when Ivor and Esme lost the first baby, it was as though the players at the Vetch rallied round, making special effort to help to compensate for the tragedy. Whether that was so, or whether it was just coincidence, the team took on a new collective confidence which was reflected in results. Between the first week in September and the beginning of December, they won nine and drew two of the eleven matches played. At the end of October, Notts County were savaged by five goals to one on their own ground, with

*The larger Academy . . . pre-season trial match.*

Ivor, who scored another 'hat-trick' , being 'the dominant figure'. He scored the first of these goals within a minute of the kick-off, and his third two minutes from the end of the game. The *Sunday Express* reported that this last goal 'was like a thunderbolt'. But, as Ivor emphasised in his newspaper column during the following week, 'It was a team performance. Brin Jones and Mel Charles dominated the middle of the field, Len (Allchurch) and Cliff (Jones) were outstanding on the wings, and Terry Medwin led the line brilliantly.' He also emphasised the part which had been played by the defence, which, he stated: 'Now that Ron Burgess has left himself out of the reckoning is marshalled by Tom Kiley.' As the weeks ahead were to show, the absence of Kiley's marshalling was to result in widespread disappointment.

Before that, though, the Swans continued to carry all before them. Even when Ivor, Cliff Jones, and Mel Charles were playing for Wales, their colleagues were far too good for their opponents. Hull City were beaten 4-1 at the Vetch and, for the first time the Swans found themselves at the top of the second-division table. At that stage, such was the level of confidence at the Vetch that, as Harry Griffiths said later, 'We felt that we could beat anyone.' And 'anyone' included a strong Liverpool side which sported in its ranks players like Moran, Saunders, Hughes, Twentyman and Liddell, who were the next visitors to Fortress Vetch Field.

Unfortunately, during the week following that fine victory, centre-half, Tom Kiley was injured in training. At Ivor's funeral in 1997, Kiley said that he had been privileged to play with a genius like Ivor and that he had been 'merely an artisan in a team of exceptional talent'. Then and later, his team-mates disagreed. To them, Tom, five or six years older than the rest, was a stabilising influence and a talisman for the younger players. Not only was his maturity an integral feature in the chemistry of the side, he became used to playing with 'adventurous wing-halves', and was a skilled reader of the game. If a team of footballers can have a collective personality, then Tom Kiley had a major influence upon that of Swansea Town at that time. As Cliff Jones put it, 'We were free to express ourselves when Tom was there.'

In Tom's absence, without a ready-made substitute to slot into the side, and in the face of the board's refusal to buy a replacement, Ron Burgess, who had not played for three months, was forced to pick himself at centre-half. Leicester City who met the Swans in the game which followed exploited the key weakness and scored six times whilst conceding just one. It was as if a bubble had burst.

Following that match, Burgess, hoping to get his board to agree to buy a replacement, sounded out all his contacts for potential recruits. There were two men on his shopping list: Bob McKinley of Nottingham Forest, who could have been bought for £10,000 and Jim Dugdale, who would have cost £7,000. Both men, Burgess understood, would have been prepared to come to Swansea at the time. Unfortunately, although attendances at the Vetch Field had risen to record levels as the side swept all before them, the board continued to intone its oft-repeated mantra: 'We do not intend to speculate. Our present policy has been shown to be sound. We will use our own resources.'

That fateful decision was to result in Swansea Town losing all but one of the next eight matches and its leadership of the Second Division. The window of opportunity had 'slammed shut'! At the end of the season, Terry Medwin, top scorer with twenty goals, asked for and was granted a transfer. For him it was the end of a dream. He asked for a transfer, he said, because he did not believe that, given the board's attitude, he would experience first-division football with Swansea Town. The directors did not try to dissuade him.

For the Swansea fans, the players, and the management team, it appeared as if the board had accepted Medwin's logic. Among those who were bitterly disillusioned by the board's negative attitude were Cliff Jones, Len Allchurch, Mel Charles, and Ivor himself. The seeds planted by that disappointment, as the future was to show, resulted in a further crop of departures from the Vetch Field. Unquestionably, the most crucial among them was to be Ivor Allchurch.

# CHAPTER FIVE

# *Exodus*

## 1956-7

Following Terry Medwin's transfer to Tottenham (for £18,000), it appeared that the Swansea Board had recognised some of the limitations of the policy which they had been following. In a foreword to the *Supporters' Club Handbook* for the 1956-7 season the chairman wrote: '. . . it does not make us overlook the fact that it takes quite a time to develop . . . young players and (as a result) . . . we may have serious gaps in our team . . . We are . . . intending to fill these gaps with players of experience . . . Swansea supporters were heartened by this news, and their joy was reinforced when another Swansea director, speaking at a function during the close season, declared: 'We are leaving no stone unturned to get the players we want before the season starts.' Even to the pessimists among the Swansea followers, these statements appeared to be unambiguously encouraging. Unfortunately, though, the subsequent actions of the board failed to match their promises. When the season started, a total of just £3,000 was all that had been spent on new men, none of whom were experienced and all of whom were to play just a handful of matches for the club. As far as many Swansea supporters were concerned, this appeared to show the members of the board in their true colours. As a result, their subsequent utterances were accepted with the same cynicism as the age-old cliché, 'White man speak with forked tongue', all too familiar to habitués of cowboy-and-Indian films of the period. The players, too, were disenchanted, and the rumblings which had affected the morale of the team during the previous campaign resurfaced. As so often happens, the departure of one employee for pastures new has a disturbing effect on those who remain. At the Vetch at the time, the failure of the board to fulfil their promises exacerbated the situation.

Nonetheless, disappointed as they were, these men were professional footballers. Furthermore, in their hearts their wish to be part of

*Captain Ivor.*

74

a team which would take Swansea into the First Division was un-diminished. And, despite Medwin's departure, there remained the nucleus of a very fine side at the Vetch.

The first three matches of the new season demonstrated this state of affairs, for all three produced victories and maximum points. The first, a five goals to one 'demolition' of Blackburn Rovers (Mel Charles scored four, and Ivor the other) was the curtain raiser, and this was followed by the defeat of Barnsley, and West Ham on their own grounds. Inexplicably, after losing the return match with Barnsley at the Vetch, the next two games were both lost. As a result, after six matches, despite the impact of the Blackburn score, the side had conceded eighteen goals whilst scoring only sixteen. Even Ivor seemed to have been affected. It was true that he missed two games because of an ankle injury, but he had scored just once during the four matches in which he had played – a poor return for him.

That ankle injury was to have another negative effect on the 'Golden Boy'. During the September of that season, rumours began to cir-culate to the effect that the Ivor-is-leaving saga was about to become a reality. At that time, the Italian football authorities had lifted their embargo on the recruitment of foreign players. As a result, so the rumour had it, Ivor Allchurch was to become the first U.K. player (after Eddie Fermani) to join an Italian club. The *Daily Mirror* re-ported that, 'Swansea Town are demanding a new British record fee of £40,000 for the services of Ivor Allchurch if he decides to quit British football.' Since the terms which were said to have been offered the player were extremely attractive, Swansea supporters feared the worst. It was reported that he would receive an £8,000 signing-on fee, his weekly salary would be double that permitted in England, and sub-stantial bonuses would be available when he played in a winning side. For the English League footballer of the period, these were riches indeed.

Not surprisingly, Ivor was besieged with enquiries from journalists and fans regarding the rumour. His response gave the Swansea fans little comfort: '. . . if the offer is as attractive as I have been told it is, I shall have to think twice before turning it down.' The Swansea chair-man added to the discomfort of the Swansea supporters when he said: 'We don't want to part with Allchurch, but, if an offer is made we should be bound to consider it. And we certainly don't want to stand in the way of a player doing well for himself.'

Reacting to this comment, the cynics declared that the second sentence in the statement was the sugar which coated the pill. Now, they argued, the board could sell the club's major asset whilst, apparently, having the player's best interests at heart. The truth fell somewhere between the two positions. There was little doubt that the board's resolve to keep Ivor had been worn down by continuing media pressure. Furthermore, the rumoured fee of £40,000 was extremely tempting to them at that time. On the other hand, there was little doubt that they did wish to do the right thing by a loyal club servant.

In the event, the rumour did not become reality. Bologna, the club said to be behind the approach, did not confirm their interest in writing. At the time, according to Swansea's Italian community, this was because the Italian club was concerned about the extent of Ivor's ankle injury. Whilst the longevity of the player's subsequent football career was to show that concern to be ill-founded, in the shorter term, Ivor missed more games that season than at any other point during his career. Apart from all this, there was another consideration which might have had an influence had an official approach been made by the Italian club.

Having in mind the desire of Swansea supporters to keep their idol at the Vetch Field, a local businessman, David Jenkins, had approached Ivor with a proposal. His idea was to open a sports shop in the town – Allchurch and Jenkins – which would provide Ivor with additional income and a business in readiness for his retirement from the game. As far as Jenkins was concerned, as he said at the time, he wasn't being altruistic, rather he was using the Allchurch name as an attraction for customers. A site was found near the town's main railway station, and the business opened in the Summer of 1956.

Ivor was delighted with the development, and greatly appreciated the support and guidance which David Jenkins gave him. It emerged, however, that the business was beset by a fundamental problem: the leading brand manufacturers at the time (following pressure from existing retailers) refused to supply the company. Nonetheless, with the business newly established, when the Italian rumour surfaced, Ivor felt obligated to David Jenkins. At the time, Jenkins sought to counsel his partner. He advised him that, if the opportunity arose, he should take it and let the Swansea business look after itself. In the event however, that contingency never arose, and not long after Ivor left for Newcastle, the 'famous brand' supply problem resulted in the business closing.

In the meantime, at the Vetch Field, the disappointing early form of the team had a negative effect on 'gate' income. For a match against Nottingham Forest at the beginning of September, 24,478 people were in the ground, whereas the 'gate' for a game with Lincoln City later that month attracted less than half that number. Not surprisingly, this was of considerable concern to the board and, apparently recognising that their no-buy policy was having a detrimental effect, they authorised Burgess to consider the purchase of new players. However, this did not placate the players, and the first of several transfer requests was made early in October. Des Palmer asked to leave and, soon after, Cliff Jones added his name to the list. Six weeks later Ivor himself asked to join them.

It was obvious to the club's supporters that these requests were indications of the dissatisfaction among the Swansea players which stemmed from the policy of the board. One result of this was that Terry Medwin's departure proved to be the precursor of a number of others. However it is arguable that, had the board acted effectively to strengthen the side after Medwin left, others might have been prepared to stay. As things turned out, the club's situation was not helped by the retirement – after a brave attempt at a 'come-back' – of the team's totem, Tom Kiley. All in all the psychological impact of these disappointments sorely bruised the ethos of the Club. Somehow, the *joie de vivre* of Swansea football was irrevocably impaired by that process. The spirit which had caused the journalist to liken the play of the team to a jihad was beginning to ebb away.

Nonetheless, with individuals of the calibre of Cliff Jones, Mel Charles, Harry Griffiths, Des Palmer, and Len and Ivor Allchurch still in the side, it was inevitable that there would be good days which helped to lift the spirits of both the team and its supporters. And, after a poor season of goal-scoring by his standards, Ivor lifted Swansea chins from Swansea chests when he scored nine goals in nine consecutive matches between December 8 and January 12, thereby setting another club record which still stands today. Unfortunately, though, two weeks later, he had a recurrence of the ankle injury which had affected him earlier in the season. As a result, Ivor missed seven consecutive matches for the Swans and was unable to play for Wales.

In retrospect, the timing of the period of inactivity may be seen to have had an influence on his eventual decision to leave the Vetch. It was the longest 'lay-off' of Ivor's career, and he had plenty of time to contemplate his position. Not having been injured to the same extent before, he came to realise, more clearly, the risks associated with the life of a professional footballer. With young John and Esme to consider, plus the attitude of the Swansea board, and his own desire to play in the top flight, the option of leaving the club appeared to be the only one open to him.

Nevertheless, looking back on the season at its end, Ivor could sustain himself with memories of games when the team had 'clicked', and the old feelings of joyous abandon had bubbled up to the surface again. The F.A. Cup match against Wolverhampton Wanderers – a leading First Division outfit of that era – was one such game. Prior to the match at Molyneaux, the press had confidently predicted a home victory. Their only misgivings sprang from the mercurial form of the Swansea side. As one writer put it, 'Brilliant one match and rubbish the next.' 'If they come off,' another scribe wrote at the time, 'they can beat any side in the land.' All warned Wolves not to be over confident and to watch Ivor, Mel Charles and Cliff Jones.

As it transpired, the home side won the match by five goals to three, but, in the process the Swans gained many new admirers. Among them were the Wolverhampton and England goalkeeper, Bert Williams, who said that he had not seen Ivor's goal as it flashed past him, and winghalf Bert Slater, who had had the task of marking the Swansea number ten. Slater declared: 'He gave me one of the toughest afternoons of my footballing life.' The Wolverhampton manager was, also, enthusiastic. 'Yes,' he said in response to a question from a journalist, 'We would be interested in signing Allchurch and one or two of the other Swansea men.' Yet again, the press joined in the 'Ivor-is-leaving' game; and, after all, his grandparents were from the Midlands, were they not?

## 1957-8

During the 1957 close-season, Ivor decided to resign the captaincy of the club. He felt that he needed to concentrate on his own fitness and form, and that a change of leader might be beneficial for the club. Ronnie Burgess tried to persuade him to change his mind, but, in the end, had to accept Ivor's argument. As far as Burgess was concerned, at least he still had Ivor in his side – *and* he was fit again.

*Ivor gets his head to the ball.*

The curtain opened on the new season with a local derby at the Ninian Park, which ended in a no-score draw. Over forty thousand people saw that match and, at the end, the press reports were unanimous in making Ivor the 'man of the match'. He was, it was noted, also one of ten Welshmen in the Swansea side, all but one of whom were born in the town. When the same Swansea side beat Lincoln City 5-1 in its next match, the optimists in Swansea began to stir, but, thereafter, it became a typical curate's egg of a season. The most depressing spell started with an October defeat at Anfield and ran for nine matches during which only one point was gained whilst thirty-two goals were conceded. Yet, during this period, six of the Swansea men were picked to play for Wales against East Germany. Although only five played, this was one indicator of the potential which remained in the Swansea side. Informed observers were convinced that with two or three additional experienced players of quality the team could mount an effective challenge for promotion to Division One. Instead, after the dismal run, they found themselves in the lower regions of the league table. Indeed, at the turn of the year, they were bottom. By then, Cliff Jones had renewed his transfer request and been joined by John King.

Ron Burgess, promised money to buy by the now beleaguered board, searched high and low without success. Either the clubs 'wanted too much money', or the players were unwilling to join a struggling club. There were no such problems in reverse. In February, Cliff Jones pressed again for a move and, within days, had joined Tottenham Hotspur for a fee of £35,000 – said, at the time, to have been a record for a winger. Ted Drake, the Chelsea manager, who had been in competition with 'Spurs for the player's signature, said that he had missed signing the best winger in the country. Whilst the Swansea fans felt proud that one of their own had attracted such praise, their pride was sullied by their disappointment. Another gem had departed. Who would be next to go?

With the possibility of relegation staring him in the face, Burgess was allowed to spend some of the money which the club had received for Jones. This time he was more successful and brought in three players, including the Welsh International centre-half, Ray Daniel, who had attended the same junior school as Ivor. Happily, the new men made an immediate difference to results, and the Swans were able to put together a series of wins. Among them was a 7-0 victory over Derby County at the Vetch, in which Ivor scored another hat-trick. He did well, too, at Grimsby in a match which the home side was expected to win.

Prior to that game, manager Burgess had told his charges to 'go for both points'. Mathematically, one point would have been enough to give them breathing space, but Burgess's psychology proved to be effective. In his report of the game, the *Sunday Express* reporter wrote, 'I have never seen Allchurch play better. No occasional bursts of speed and enthusiasm for him – for fully ninety minutes he plotted and planned Grimsby's downfall and tackled with a venom usually associated with a full-back.' Several other papers echoed these sentiments. As the *People* reporter put it in describing one incident, 'In the end Allchurch decided to go it alone. He beat two Grimsby defenders and, a yard outside the penalty area, he was tripped by the home centre-half. The Swansea man took the kick himself, and the Grimsby 'keeper did not move as it screamed past him into the net.'

By this time, Mel Nurse (Ivor's self-appointed batman) had won a place in the Swansea first team. Mel Charles, remembering that trip to Grimsby, recalled an example of Nurse's devotion. In the mid-fifties such a journey involved two changes of train and, for the last leg of the trip, the players found themselves in a non-corridor coach. As the train wound its way towards its destination, there were those among the occupants of that compartment who felt 'peckish'. When the subject was raised, Nurse took a packet of 'Nippets' from his pocket, gave one of the little liquorice sweets to Ivor and returned the packet to his pocket. No one else was offered a sweet, but, so well known was the youngster's adulation of Ivor that the other players accepted the situation with raucous good humour.

When the curtain came down on what had been a difficult campaign, despite having missed a quarter of the season's games, Ivor's name topped the list of leading scorers. It was another testimony of his worth to the Swansea club, and was one of the reasons why the team was able to look forward to second-division football for the 1958-9 season. But that was not what Ivor wanted. His goal was Division One, and, as things stood, it seemed to him to be unlikely that, at his age, he would gain that status at the Vetch Field. Those who remembered his statements over the years called to mind that he had said, 'If I cannot get first-division football at the Vetch, I shall have to look elsewhere.' As they contemplated the season ahead, some supporters buried their heads in the sands of optimism; the realists, however, began to prepare themselves for what they saw as the inevitable.

## 1958-9

It was the view of the realists which was boosted by events before the new campaign began. During the close-season, the chairman announced that the club had too many players, and eleven of them were 'listed' as being available for transfer. Among those who left at the time of the announcement were Brin Jones, Cliff's brother, and Dudley Peake. Others were to follow but, in the meantime, a decision which was to change the playing ethos of the Vetch Field club was made public by the chairman. The club was to appoint a General Manager.

At the end of June, the former Cardiff City manager, Trevor Morris, was appointed to the post. Although no one had made clear what the general manager's role involved, there were those who interpreted it

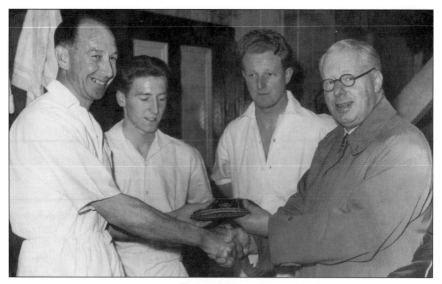

*Congratulations . . .*
*Ronnie Burgess, Cliff Jones, Ivor and Chairman, Philip Holden, and 'Cap'.*

as being concerned with the business management of the club. In the event, however, it became clear that Morris envisaged his task as including team management. Since Ron Burgess believed that this was to be his domain, the former 'Spur' asked the board for clarification. That clarification resulted in Burgess's resignation. He was not, he said, prepared to accept the role of Assistant Manager.

Given that Ivor and the majority of the other players had enjoyed considerable rapport with Burgess in the way he wanted to play football, they viewed his departure with regret. No longer, they believed, could they look forward to playing the type of game in which they could 'express themselves', for rumour had it that Trevor Morris was a 'system' man. It was said that the adventurous spirit personified by the Burgess-Sykes-Allchurch triumvirate would be frowned upon. And so it transpired, for Morris was an earnest student of football tactics. The structure and methods which he introduced were the precursor of the football play today. '4-4-2' and the like became the *lingua franca* of the game, and Morris talked about the 'Barcelona formation'.

In retrospect, it could be argued that the time when Morris arrived was a watershed in football tactics, and that the traditional British style of play was yielding place to the influences of Spain, South America and Italy. Certainly, these influences gripped the British game with remarkable speed. Indeed, the manager of Newcastle, the club which Ivor was to join on leaving he Vetch, was an advocate of the Barcelona approach. At the Vetch, however, the departure of Burgess and the demotion of Joe Sykes to 'look after the youngsters', was seen by the man-in-the-street and the players alike as a statement of a more cautious intent. The *joie de vivre*, the jihad approach, and the 7-3 games with clubs like Fulham, were to be things of the past.

Nevertheless, there were more than twenty thousand people at the Vetch to see the side win its first home match against Scunthorpe, and five thousand more to see Fulham win by two goals to one. After six matches, however, there was little evidence that the Morris systems were being effective. Two of these games had been won, three lost and one drawn. It was hardly promotion form, though, in fairness, a fundamental change in the style of play takes time to achieve. The next match, however, resulted in a win which gave the supporters great comfort. Sunderland, a club which had been relegated from the First Division at the end of the previous season, were the opponents at the Vetch Field, and they fielded players of the calibre of Revie, Hedley, and Hurley. Morris drafted 17-year-old Herbie Williams (the 'new Ivor') in at inside-right for his début. And what an experience it was for the boy!

The *South Wales Evening Post* headline for its report of that match read: 'SWANS WHIP ALL STARS', though not all the stars were listed on the Sunderland team sheet. The outstanding player on view that day was Ivor Allchurch, who helped himself to four of the five goals scored by the Swans. In scoring these goals, he demonstrated his range of skills yet again. The first was a well-placed header, the second was converted from just two yards, the third a 'twenty-yard rocket', and the fourth resulted from an amazing dribbling surge which seemed to take him past five Sunderland men before crashing the ball into the net.

But, after the Lord Mayor's show . . . Following a 0-0 draw at Leyton Orient, the next match, at Stoke, was lost (though Ray Daniel was injured). By that time it was obvious that the side needed strengthening, and Morris, in response to a question from a Swansea journalist, Bill Paton, said: 'I am well aware of what I want. The board are behind me and are prepared to allow me to spend a five-figure sum to get the right men.' Reading this, the cynics in Swansea not unnaturally wondered where the board would get the money? After all, this was the same group of men who had said that the club had to reduce the number of players on its staff, and who, In the past, had been unwilling to spend significant sums. Was someone else about the leave? The tea leaf readers had no doubt what the outcome would be.

At the end of September less than twenty thousand people were in the Vetch to see the match with Charlton Athletic. Whether this reduction in 'gate' reflected the relative lack of success of the side or whether it was the style of play, can only be a matter of conjecture. Whatever the reason, 19,520 people witnessed what, in the annals of the Vetch Field story can only be regarded as an historic match. They were to see Ivor play for the Swans for the last time before he insisted on being made available for transfer, and they were to see the name 'Allchurch I.', put into the referee's book for the only time; his misdemeanour was to stand too close to the ball at a free kick. In addition, they saw Ivor score what was to be his last goal for the Swans in second-division football.

There was, too, another point of discussion on the Tanner Bank. The 'Golden Boy' did not come out for the second half, because, it was reported, he had strained a thigh muscle. In those days, before substitutes were allowed, it was usual for an injured player to make as much of a nuisance of himself as possible on the left wing. Had they been able to see the headlines during the week ahead the Swansea fans might well have made two plus two equal five. Was Trevor Morris, they might have asked, making sure that the player was physically fit to be transferred?

Although it has not been possible to establish all the facts, there is sufficient evidence to suggest that, early in his time at the Vetch, Trevor Morris had decided to part with Ivor and use the money received to strengthen the side. Unlike his predecessors, Morris had business experience, could 'wheel and deal' with the best, and was able to liaise with the board on equal terms. Certainly, Morris gave Ivor the impression that, if he wanted to leave, the board would not stand in his way. Furthermore, Morris had established the availability of both Colin Webster and Reg Davies before brokering the Allchurch deal. It was all too structured to be accidental, and, as far as Ivor was concerned, was the stimulus which, finally, made him leave the Vetch for Division One.

*Airborne Ivor.*

On October 2 the newspapers reported that Ivor was to leave the Vetch. Numerous clubs were said to be negotiating for him, including Newcastle United, Aston Villa, Birmingham, Manchester United and the Wolves. Newcastle was the first club to put in a bid, offering £18,000 plus a player. Morris sat on his hands as the others considered their positions. The manager of Liverpool, then in the Second Division, said that he and his chairman would charter a plane and fly down at Swansea's behest, meeting the Vetch club's valuation. Ivor, however, would only move to the First Division. On October 4 Middlesboro' joined the would-be bidders.

Meantime, Ivor had spoken frankly to Bill Paton, a journalist who had reported on the player's progress since his early days at the Vetch. He confessed:

> 'At twenty-eight, it's now or never. I've thought about it a great deal and, but for our precarious position last season, I would have pressed for my release then.'

Then, in his own column in the *South Wales Evening Post*, Ivor wrote:

'I am sure that it did not come as a surprise to Mr. Morris that I want to go. I am ready to admit that I had hopes that my own club would get promotion a couple of years ago . . . then I would have been happy to end my career in the town . . . But that dream does not look like coming true.'

By October 8, Aston Villa had made a firm bid for Ivor's services, but Newcastle, through their chairman, Alderman McKeag, came back with an increased offer. Whilst it was reported that the Newcastle board was 'split' on whether to pay such a large sum for a twenty-eight year-old, McKeag backed his manager, Charlie Mitten.

Two days later, Ivor Allchurch caught a train to Manchester to meet with Mitten, though Esme remembers that he did not take his boots with him, because he said, he was not going to be rushed into making a decision. In the event, however, Charlie Mitten's 'sales pitch' won Ivor over. The 'Golden Boy' signed forms on a railway parcels trolley at Manchester Exchange Station, sent for his boots, was on the way to Newcastle with his new manager, and was ready to play on the following day.

Meantime, Trevor Morris, in addition to selling Ivor, on the same day, signed both Colin Webster and Reg Davies, sold Pat Terry, and according to Bill Paton, 'Beamed all over his face'. He had bought two internationals for a total of £11,000, and was £21,000 in credit. The Swansea chairman, Philip Holden was impressed enough to telephone his congratulations on deals well done. None of this was to Ivor's detriment. Both Swansea men said that they were sorry to see him go. Yet 'business is business' and no one could argue other than that Morris had been an effective negotiator. Even from where Ivor stood, the arrangements could be viewed with some pleasure. He had achieved his goal of first-division football whilst providing his hometown club with the financial where-with-all to take them forward. It was a satisfactory outcome for both clubs. The thousands of Swansea supporters who idolised Ivor however, were left with deep feelings of sadness. The 'Golden Boy' was theirs no more.

# CHAPTER SIX

# The 1958 World Cup

To play in the World Cup Finals is the ambition of every footballer. That ambition, world-wide as it is, has a particular resonance in small nations, where players and even supporters fantasise about scoring a winning goal in the World Cup Final to defeat either the Brazilians or the mighty Germans. Everyone who follows football cherishes dreams, but occasionally there are moments of real achievement, which serve to legitimise such fantasies. Only once has Wales, a country with fewer than three million inhabitants, qualified for the World Cup finals and the team's performances during that competition were not at all bad. Certainly, they were sufficiently good to encourage all kinds of wishful speculation. Wales did not win the World Cup in Sweden in 1958 but they progressed further than the much more highly rated Scotland and England teams. In fact, the Welsh and the Northern Ireland teams became the first United Kingdom representatives in history to reach the quarter-finals of the competition. Furthermore, it looked for a while as if Wales could make it to the semi-final, and, if that had happened, then all kinds of speculation would have been permissible. In that very honourable and memorable progression, Ivor Allchurch played a crucial role.

It must be admitted at the outset that, as we have seen in chapter 3, Wales only made it to Sweden through the back door. What is more, the opportunism with which the Welsh F.A. responded to the chance to meet Israel in that one-off home and away tie did not please everyone. Brian Glanville in the *Sunday Times* took a dim view of this lucky break and he made the contrast with Uruguay who had been surprisingly eliminated by Paraguay. Proudly, Glanville pompously declared, 'Uruguay refused a second chance. Wales were not so proud.'

Back door entry it might have been, but Wales took the chance boldly. The team travelled to Tel Aviv in January 1958 for what was to be their first game ever outside Europe. They were visiting a troubled land, and Peter Corrigan spoke of the tank tracks on the pitch and of

*The Wales side which played Israel at Cardiff to book a World Cup place.*
*Back row: Alan Harrington, Stuart Williams, John Charles, Jack Kelsey, Mel Hopkins, Ivor Allchurch, Mel Charles.*
*Front row: Terry Medwin, Ron Hewitt, Dave Bowen, Cliff Jones.*

refugees being moved out of the dressing rooms. But Wales were given a warm welcome and the fixture caught the imagination of the young Israelis and has lived on in the memory. At the time, the Israelis looked forward to the tussle between their amateurs, in particular, the 17 year-old Gideon Tisch and the great John Charles – about whom they had read so much. For years thereafter there was talk in Tel Aviv and Jerusalem of Charles, 'The Prince of Wales'. There was talk too of Chodorov, the home-team's goalkeeper, who performed acrobatically. In his novel *The Book of Intimate Grammar*, David Grossman has the young Aron imitating for a month 'Chodorov's save from the game against Wales, where the goalkeeper dives parallel to the ground and blocks a "howitzer" shot from right field'. That shot was, almost certainly, from Ivor Allchurch, whose performance that day gave Chodorov every chance to shine. The keeper, however, could only 'gulp in alarm' in the 38th minute when Ivor 'atomised the ball', and placed his left-foot drive in the corner of the net. It was this goal that 'cracked Israel' and, in the words of Gwilym Evans, 'virtually stamped Welsh passports for the World Cup Finals'. A crowd of 55,000, which included about 100 Welsh soldiers from Cyprus, had come to see the great John Charles who was rated as a £75,000 player but said Evans, Ivor, who had cost the Swans just £10.0s.0d, was 'today's 5-star artist'. This was Ivor's 'dream come-back' after a period of personal frustration. Evans called for 'Cheers from the Welsh Valleys please, because Ivor Allchurch is back at his breezy, brilliant best'. In Tel Aviv, Wales won 2-0, and that scoreline was repeated three weeks later at Ninian Park when Allchurch again scored the opener. Bags for Sweden could be packed.

In Fleet Street there was not a little disquiet and misgiving about Wales going to Sweden, but at least there was solace in the possibility that the tournament would allow reporters to catch glimpses of John Charles who was now being regularly talked of as one of the most exciting players in the world. That this was only a possibility was down to the Italian Football Federation. In April 1957, Charles had been transferred from Leeds to Juventus of Turin for £65,000, and, thereupon a struggle commenced for the F.A. of Wales. Traditionally they had found it difficult to obtain the release of players; Charles included, from English clubs. Now it was considerably more difficult to get their star player away from Turin when key matches were played. Wales had played three matches before the two Israel games without Charles, and, right up to the last minute, there were doubts as to whether he would make it to Stockholm. Even with their star player, Wales were given little chance by the pundits; without him they were thought of as a bit of a joke.

Charles was undoubtedly the man of the moment at the time. Already football writers were waxing eloquent about this wholly re-markable figure that had emerged from the back streets of Swansea. Everything about him was different. At six-feet-two and fourteen stone and with his swarthy appearance he looked more like the hero of an Italian epic movie than a footballer. Yet this 'Gentle Giant', who could dominate at centre-half or intimidate at centre-forward, was never booked and very rarely infringed any rule because everything he did win was characterised by grace and delicacy. He was a godsend not just to British, but to world football and quite naturally he had been snapped up by one of the most fanatical of all soccer cities. In his first season at Juventus he scored sensational 28 goals and was immed-iately idolised. The man who had gone as a sixteen-year-old from Swansea to Leeds had found a true home in Turin where he reigned supreme for five years. Meanwhile, this Italian dimension exacerbated what was, in truth, something of a dilemma for Welsh officials. Of course, Charles was idolised by Wales too, where he had first worn his national colours as an eighteen-year-old in 1950. Throughout the decade there had been first the question of whether he would be available, and, if he turned out, there was the agonising decision as to where to play him. Before Charles went to Stockholm he had played for Wales on twenty-five occasions; in twelve games he had been listed at centre-half, in thirteen at centre forward. Of course, plans were not always adhered to and frequently he had been switched during games, dropping back to defend a lead, or going forward to snatch a winner. All the while there was the further awkward question of whether his presence affected other players and somewhat distorted the natural Welsh game. For many years he had somewhat boxed and coxed with Trevor Ford, a great centre-forward in his own right, who didn't really need another, mightier presence. By the time of the Swedish games, Ford had gone but there was still the question of Ivor whose game had its own pattern and rhythm and which created its own logic. Pick-ing the Welsh team was no easy matter.

The man who had to deal with these dilemmas was the marvellous Jimmy Murphy, who in 1956 had succeeded Walley Barnes to become the second manager of the Welsh team. Deservedly Murphy, Rhondda-Irish through and through, is a football legend. After a League career at West Brom, and fifteen caps as an attacking half-back, he had served as a sergeant in the wartime Eighth Army. Whilst serving in Italy he met Matt Busby, who took him to Manchester United first as a coach and then as assistant manager. The highly-publicised and much admired 'Busby Babes' were, in part, the 'Murphy Babes', for at Old Trafford Jimmy had particular responsibility for the youngsters and rising stars, who Eamon Dunphy has made clear, owed him a great deal. Murphy was the great motivator. Harry McShane remembered him as a 'very aggressive character, always het-up, a typical Welsh-man', who could often be heard shouting through the dressing room wall 'Get bloody stuck in'. Nobby Stiles recalled Jimmy's emphasis on 'fire in your belly', and on the value of United's red shirts which were 'the best in the world'; 'when you put that on nothing can beat you!'

Murphy was at Old Trafford for a quarter of a century but above all it was his contribution in that fateful year of 1958 that will be lovingly remembered. He was not on the plane that crashed at Munich because he was with the Welsh team who were playing Israel at Cardiff. Subsequently at Old Trafford, with Matt Busby in hospital, he had to take up the reins. That season, he took his cruelly deprived United team to the F.A. Cup Final. That over he could switch his attention to his other job. Would Charles be available? What team should he pick? In 1958 nobody in the football world was as busy or as pre-occupied as Jimmy Murphy, Manager of Wales.

Murphy took stock of his team at Roehampton where a practice game was played against England. Clearly, much was going to depend on John Charles, who was obviously destined to play up-front, for the manager was seen walking the touch line crying out for high crosses. The team then travelled to their base at Sandviken, an industrial town 120 miles north of Stockholm. Confidence was developing apace especially after a local team, Soltsjobaden, were beaten 19-0 in a practice match, Allchurch scoring seven and Charles five. The big man had bruised a knee in the game and did only light training. He hoped that Wales would win, 'but, otherwise, expected an England v. Russia final'. The Welsh captain, Arsenal's Dave Bowen was more up-beat, and re-ported on how 'spirit had improved considerably' since the arrival of John Charles. Team members later recalled that everyone had joined in a chorus of 'For he's a jolly good fellow', as Big John had walked into the Welsh hotel with his Juventus minder. 'We are full of beans,' Bowen said, 'and we expect to win.'

Bowen was a key figure in the Welsh team. A classy and intelligent player, he was a born leader for whom as Peter Corrigan has shown, Jimmy Murphy had tremendous respect. Goals, it was hoped, would come from Charles, and it was up to the other forwards like Allchurch to feed him. Meanwhile there would be lots of defending to be done and in this respect Bowen would be vital, for the system to be adopted was the Arsenal 'Funnel' method which involved everyone dropping back. The skipper's task was to muster his relatively untried defensive line-up. At full-back were Stuart Williams and Mel Hopkins, who had both been around for a couple of season, though they had only played in harness five times. Bowen himself had eleven caps and alongside him in the half-back line were John Charles's younger brother, Mel who had played three more games, and Derek Sullivan who had been in and out of the Welsh team during a five-year period in which he had won nine caps, and who came in to replace his injured Cardiff team-mate, Alan Harrington. In terms of British football, this was not a star-studded line-up; these were not defenders who were mentioned in Wales in the same breath as Barnes, Burgess, Sherwood and Daniel. The one great consolation was that Arsenal's Jack Kelsey would be in goal. Kelsey to perform miracles whilst at the other end Charles would head in from a cross or a corner. That was the basic Welsh master-plan.

Wales found themselves in Group Three, along with Mexico, the host nation, Sweden, and the mighty Hungarians, who five years earlier after they had revolutionised the world of football by their perfor-mance at Wembley, and who still had great stars like Sandor and Hidegkuti in their line-up. In their three group games Wales, accord-ing to Geoffrey Green, the doyen of soccer pundits, were disappoint-ing. The Welsh camp themselves saw it rather differently, for there had been encouraging moments and, above all, the team was still in the competition. The opening game, against Hungary, was played in front of a crowd of 17,000 at a pleasant rural stadium at Sandviken. The result was a 1-1 draw, but it was a match the Welsh camp felt they should have won. Initially, Wales, playing in an unfamiliar yellow, had been outplayed after Hungary had taken an early lead. Then in the 26th minute Cliff Jones took a corner and from it Charles rising well above a crowd of defenders scored one of his 'special' headers. Wales, now fought their way back into what had become a thrilling encounter which both sides came close to winning. At first Ivor had been uncertain, but he found his pace in the second half and was soon testing Grosics in the Hungarian goal. What the Welsh team thought was the decisive moment came in the 71st minute, when a precision pass from John Charles allowed Ivor to swoop for goal only to be brought down in the area by a 'violent back charge'. Later, the Hungarian manager claimed that his defender, Matrai, 'had played the ball first'. The reporter, Bob McGowran reckoned that of all those in the stadium only the Uruguayan referee shared that interpretation. Throughout the game both Allchurch and Charles had been roughly handled, but, disappointingly, Charles had made nothing of six free kicks taken from the edge of the penalty area.

Nevertheless all the post-match talk had been of Charles, and clearly he was already the most feared player in the tournament. Already too, a great deal more was being expected of Wales generally. Meanwhile there was a problem to be sorted out in the Welsh camp. Sullivan had injured a knee, and yet another Cardiff halfback, Colin Baker, was brought into the team to gain his first cap in the match against Mexico. There had been some dissatisfaction with the performance of the forward line. Terry Medwin, the Spurs winger, had not been particularly effective playing out of position at inside right and the Welsh were beginning to believe that it was perhaps a mistake to concentrate exclusively on getting the ball to John Charles. In a perceptive analysis, Tony Pawson suggested that 'the present of Charles seemed to awe his colleagues' so that 'even great players like Ivor Allchurch appeared to shrink in stature, as if so dwarfed by him mentally and physically, that they mistrusted their own powers'. To Pawson the other forwards around Charles seemed 'like minor executives hurrying about their business and avoiding contact with the formidable managing director.' There was talk of the problems, but nothing was done and in the next match Wales were very lucky to draw 1-1 with Mexico, a game played in a half-empty Stockholm stadium. The Welsh heroes were all in defence. Even John Charles confessed that he 'was bad tonight'. He blamed himself, though it was noted that he did not receive one decent pass. The forward line in general was described as being 'ragged and aimless' with only Ivor showing to any effect. All the fireworks had come from him; at one point or other, he hit the bar, posts and side netting with shots or free kicks, and in the 22nd minute had given

Wales the lead by driving the ball through the legs of defenders and past the unsighted 'keeper. In an 'unbearably exciting finish' the Mexicans kept people waiting until near the end before equalising, but it was a goal that was bound to come. Wales had been as bad as they have previously been good. 'Football's a funny game', was Murphy's verdict.

The next match against Sweden was an even greater disappointment. The host nation, which had already qualified for the knock-out stage, took the opportunity to blood several young reserves but Wales failed to take advantage and, indeed, at times looked as if they were incapable of doing so. They played like a side that knew all too well that a draw would keep them in the competition by taking them to a play-off game. They sat back and defended, with Charles briefly dropping back to forage, and, in effect, becoming a second centre-half alongside brother Mel. Even then it took valiant efforts from Kelsey and Stuart Williams to keep Wales in a game which ended goal-less. A new-look forward line which included Roy Vernon and Cardiff's Ron Hewitt was better balanced, though again Ivor had been the 'star'. According to Bob McGowran he 'was always scheming and striving' and was 'unlucky with his shooting'. The manager had spotted that he was the only forward who was 'hitting the ball hard', and he was under orders to 'keep shooting' whilst others did the 'fetching and carrying'. It was a role which he would fulfil again later in his career.

Despite their problems, with both England and Scotland on their way home, the Welsh took pride and pleasure in their growing team spirit and effectiveness as a unit. This was important to them as they prepared for their play-off match against Hungary. The World Cup venture which had started in Tel Aviv was just going on and on. As Dave Bowen proudly pointed out, Jimmy Murphy's record spoke for itself. Under him Wales had lost only one of their ten matches and had conceded just five goals. As a result some people were beginning to wonder whether Wales needed to fear any of the other teams left in the competition. In the short-term, though, what they had to fear was Hungarian tackling, for, unfortunately, the play-off was a brutal affair. For Geoffrey Green, the Hungarian tactics were 'questionable' and they were rightly booed off the field. Tony Pawson was even more outspoken, condemning their 'vicious' tackles and their 'despicable' tactics of shackling John Charles by 'whatever means – however illegal'. Charles was hacked down so often that it was hardly surprising that he pulled a leg muscle in the second half. Ron Hewitt, who had earlier charged the 'keeper was also picked on and was eventually carried off. One Hungarian defender was sent off, but this was the only response of the Russian referee. Several commentators noted that only twenty-four hours before the game with Wales, Imre Nagy, the leader of the Hungarian Rising, had been executed. With some Hungarian supporters wearing black this was no time for a Russian to treat Hungarian players severely.

Wales responded to all this quite magnificently. They all showed annoyance, even the normally placid Charles, but they kept their heads and the match was won in style. A brilliant Tichy goal had given Hungary a first half lead, but Kelsey had kept it at 1-0. In the second half, the Welsh forwards, with Charles and Medwin playing well, developed a 'dynamic surge' which inevitably brought goals from two long-range shots. The second of these was scored by Medwin; the first by Allchurch constituted what was, without doubt, the highlight of the whole Welsh experience in that World Cup.

Earlier, Bob McGowron had noted that Allchurch was 'brilliantly turning on a sixpence' either to create openings or to fire in sizzling shots. Then in the 56th minute, standing on the angle of the penalty area, he received a long, lobbed pass from John Charles, 'and, without waiting for the ball to hit the ground, he hit it on the volley with his left foot'. According to McGowron it streaked into the net with such ferocious speed that Grosics didn't see it; it was 'as grand a shot as you would see in a month of Sundays'. Tony Pawson noted that the lob from the hobbling Charles was perfect; he then saw Ivor 'eager as a whippet' . . . 'streak in on the ball and smash a volley into the net'. That great equaliser, was the turning point of the match. Many thought that this was the goal of the tournament, later one historian termed it as 'perhaps the greatest shot ever seen in the World Cup'. Just three days later Wales had to play the biggest game in its history as a foot-balling nation, a quarter-final match against the tournament favourites Brazil.

The match was lost that day in Gothenburg, but the Welsh team earned many plaudits and won admirers. Brazil, of course, went on to win the competition and in so doing they not only became the first winners of the World Cup to triumph on an alien continent, but they also began an era of dominance in which their brand of 'total football' set entirely new standards of skill and entertainment. In Sweden in

1958 the world was introduced to a new set of stars, including Mazzola, Didi and above all the winger Garrincha, whom Geoffey Green was to project as the 'Stanley Matthews of the New World'. Also in the Brazilian line-up was the seventeen-year-old Edson Arantes do Nascimento, known to the world, if not to his family, as Pelé. And it was he who, having started the tournament as a reserve, forced his way into the Brazilian team in time to score a lucky winner against Wales.

Brazil had gone into the game with many advantages. They were playing their fourth game at the Villen stadium, they had rested for five days as compared with their opponents' three, and they were facing a Welsh side which had been cruelly deprived of both John Charles and Ron Hewitt. Nevertheless, Wales held out for over 70 minutes until, from a Garrincha cross, Pelé sent in a close-range shot which ricocheted off Stuart Williams's heel to roll agonisingly slowly past the scrambling and blameless Kelsey. It was an unsatisfactory way for Wales to lose, for on the day they were, in the words of McGowran 'unbowed and far from disgraced'; 'they fought to the last ditch'. And things so easily could have gone the other way, for although 'Allchurch was too closely shadowed to pull off the juggling tricks of earlier matches', he had skimmed the post in the 36th minute. Of course, all the speculation centred on what Wales would have done if John Charles had been able to play. Meanwhile, all the plaudits went to a Welsh defence that Brian Glanville described as 'masterful'. For Geoffrey Green, Jack Kelsey's performance had been 'flawless'; Bob McGowron's hero was Mel Charles, who, he thought, 'had done the work of two men'.

Looking back at these events, Welsh fans are fully aware that they need to keep a sense of perspective with regard to the events of June 1958. The team was lucky to have been in Sweden at all, they did not win a Group match, they only scored four goals in five games and there was to be some criticism of their negative tactics and excessive caution. Some modesty is in order, but so, too, is some pride. The play-off game against Hungary should never be forgotten. 'This was the glory of Wales', said Tony Pawson who 'from drab beginnings and dreary opposition' saw the team 'fashion a match as dramatic and thrilling as any I have ever seen'.

Furthermore, throughout the tournament, Welsh players were talked about at some length both in the press and in opposing training camps. Everyone, of course, talked about the great John Charles and wondered how he would be deployed. In fact, even before his injury, the Juventus man had not really been at his best, as Geoffrey Green acknowledged. Nonetheless, Green went on to conclude that, 'This Goliath among men and footballer of calm authority' would 'still win a place in the world side of any generation.' The headlines were always dominated by John Charles, but the real hero of 1958 was playing a little more anonymously in defence, for many keen observers had noted the world-class displays of the younger Charles brother, Swansea Town's Mel.

Of the Welsh forwards it was undoubtedly Ivor Allchurch who caught the eye of informed observers. He had scored two goals, one of them particularly memorable, and had come tantalisingly close to scoring two more. His contribution to the Welsh cause, though, was greater than that for it was said that throughout the time in Sweden he had inspired his side 'through his authority and dignity of bearing'. Ivor had found his true level and it was his natural authority in this exalted company which allowed his team as a whole to settle. 'We surprised a lot of people,' recalled Dave Bowen, 'they looked at Ivor and wondered where he had been hiding.' Brazil were in the process of discovering a new Number 10 in Pelé, but Bowen was not alone in suggesting that Allchurch could have worn that particular Brazilian shirt with distinction. 'He could have played for any of the teams,' argued Bowen. That was Jimmy Murphy's view too. For him it had been a tournament of great players, there had been much talk of Pelé, Didi and Kopa, but, said the Welsh manager 'the greatest inside-forward in the World Cup was Ivor Allchurch'. As the Welsh contribution to the tournament ended, Jimmy Murphy was joined by the great Señor Bernabeu of Real Madrid who, nodding at Allchurch, asked if he could have the autograph 'of the greatest inside-forward in the world'.

The teams went home; John Charles to Turin, Jimmy Murphy to Old Trafford and Jack Kelsey and Dave Bowen to Highbury. For Ivor Allchurch and Mel Charles, though, it was back to training at the Vetch Field. Eight weeks after the Gothenburg match they were both in the Swansea Town side that lost to Sheffield Wednesday in a second-division game.

CHAPTER SEVEN

# *Wor Ivor*

*1958-9*

When he arrived in Newcastle on that October Friday in 1958, Ivor did not know a great deal about the place. He had played at St. James's Park in the F.A. Cup in front of 61,000 people, and was aware that United was a big club in every sense. He remembered that his former team-mate, Tom Kiley, who had relatives in the area, had told him that 'it was an overcoat colder up there', but that 'the warmth of the people made up for it'. Ivor confirmed for himself the truth of both these comments, and, in particular, quickly made friends in a community which, he always said, was 'just like Swansea'.

Not surprisingly, he knew little about the football club, other than being aware that it was rooted in a hotbed of football fanaticism, and that it had had a magnificent team which had won the F.A. Cup in the early fifties. That achievement had made the names Jackie Milburn, Frank Brennan, Ronnie Simpson, and the like, well-known to him, and in particular, he knew of the legend of 'Wor Jackie'. When, in due course, the Geordie fans, warming to his skills and demeanour, called him 'Wor Ivor', he took it as a tremendous compliment. In Swansea he had been 'Our Ivor', but since he had been born there, the pronoun 'our' had been an instinctive expression of his membership of the extended family of the town. That, of course, was not the case in Newcastle, yet the Geordie fans 'adopted' him with an alacrity which suggested some kind of spiritual kinship. Consequently, the tag 'Wor Ivor' became as natural to those Newcastle supporters as if he had been Tyneside-born.

At the time of his arrival at St. James's Park, there had been much comment in the Newcastle press about the lack of unity within the Newcastle board. It was said to be bedevilled by two rival factions constantly at loggerheads. Charlie Mitten had told Ivor that there had been 'some bickering' within the board about signing him, but that the Chairman, Alderman McKeag, was fully supportive of the decision, and 'He was the man who mattered'. What Ivor did not know at the time was that the factions were prepared to disagree about almost anything. In that sense, even if he had not been reassured by Mitten, he need not have been concerned that half the board believed that they should have signed a younger player. From the outset, the quality of his performances on the field, plus his bearing and the palpable honesty of his endeavour, quickly endeared him to fans and directors alike.

As Paul Jounnou records in his definitive *'Newcastle United – a complete record 1882-1986'*, that powerful rapport was maintained throughout Ivor's time at St. James's Park:

'His all-round ability made him almost worth two lesser players. He was considered the perfect footballer, with his leisurely manner perhaps disguising his great skills. United have probably never fielded a better schemer in post-war football. Allchurch possessed superb passing ability and could hit unerringly accurate long or short passes equally well either foot . . . (he) rarely had an indifferent game for United.'

*The Début*

Since Ivor was signed by Newcastle on the day before the match with Leicester in October 1958, he did not meet his new team-mates until the morning of his début. It followed that he was not *au fait* with their style of play, nor with their strengths and weaknesses. Mitten had given him a verbal briefing about the other players, but Ivor was keen to find out for himself what they were really like. He was aware, however, that Newcastle had spent, what was then, a significant sum of money in signing him. Consequently, despite his vast experience in International football, it was not surprising that, after the game, he confessed to feeling 'a little nervous' as he ran out onto the St. James's Park pitch to make his first-division début.

Not that the circumstances can have worried him unduly. As he said: 'The reception which the Geordie fans gave me made me feel at home at once!' Indeed, so much 'at home' did he feel, that, after just eight minutes of the match, that warm welcome was superseded by a

*Newcastle United, 1958-9.*
Back row (left to right): J. Scoular, J. Nesbitt, R. Stokoe, R. Simpson, R. Keith, A. McMichael,
A. Franks. Front row: W. Wright, G. Eastham, L. White, K. Hale, R. Mitchell.
*Inset: I. Allchurch.*

deafening, ecstatic roar of delight from the Newcastle supporters. The report in the paper that 'The Welshman crashed home an unstoppable free-kick from two yards outside the penalty box', hardly did justice to the goal that delighted those Geordie fans, nor to the deeper feelings that it generated.

Ivor had 'arrived', and the Newcastle supporters had begun the process of taking the former Swansea man to their collective bosom. They had worshiped great players before; they had heard about others; and they had seen numerous men come to Newcastle but fail to fulfil the promise of greatness which had been attached to them. Knowledgeable about the game as they were, the Gallowgate faithful knew that true greatness resides in exceptionally few footballers. When the final whistle went that day, however, they were certain that they had glimpsed it in their new golden-haired inside-forward from Wales.

That Saturday night, the headline in the *Newcastle Chronicle* trumpeted:

'It's "Ivor" United', and the paper's match report left its readers in no doubt about the quality of the Magpies' newest recruit. 'Newcastle can be well satisfied with the bumper cheque they have paid . . . (for) Allchurch . . . he showed the stamp of a brilliant footballer . . . He was the outstanding home forward.'

Not surprisingly, manager, Charlie Mitten was delighted with the début performance of his new player. Ivor had answered those critics who had argued that £28,000 was far too much to pay for a player approaching his twenty-ninth birthday. The player had established an immediate rapport with the fans, and he had enriched the Eastham-White partnership to such an extent that Mitten believed that he now possessed the best strike trio in British football. And given that the three men registered 48 of the 81 goals scored by the 'Magpies' during that season, his judgement could hardly be faulted. Mitten was also well aware of the fact that, despite having missed twenty-five per cent of the campaign, Ivor finished the season as second-top scorer with sixteen goals. The manager and the Newcastle faithful knew that they had a player who could score, often spectacular, goals as well as scheme.

Throughout that first season at St. James's Park, many of Ivor's performances gave the Geordie fans much delight. However, the Welshman's efforts in two matches during his first seven months at the club stood out. The first was in a 4-0 drubbing of Everton, and the second a 4-4 draw with Manchester United at Old Trafford two weeks later.

The Everton match took place in freezing conditions which proved to be a stern test of ball-control and technique. Ivor, however, rose above it all. A report in the *Empire News* reflected the way in which he weaved his magic into the occasion:

'The United fans have never seen Allchurch quite so brilliantly commanding. Long passes to the wings made one gasp with admiration of sheer perfection of "strength". Even Shackleton never entertained more pawkily than did Ivor, as he shuffled the ball across and around a "sixpence" to the bewilderment of three or four challengers.'

*The People*, after following a similar line of worshipful awe, reminded its readers of the all-round ability of the Newcastle number 8 (McGuigan played at inside-left that day):

'He scored with a rocket-like header from behind the penalty spot – Jackie Milburn would have been delighted with that!'

That day, the press and the fans were in unison. They rose to the Welshman *en bloc*, whilst another famous footballing name was added to the growing army of Allchurch-admirers. George Hardwick wrote:

'I consider Manager Mitten's signing of Welsh star, Ivor Allchurch to be one of the best moves of the football season.'

Even the factions on the Newcastle board found it difficult to disagree over that verdict.

It was the away match against Manchester United, however, which most football *aficionados* believed to be the pinnacle of that first Allchurch season at Newcastle. The headlines were strident: 'Allchurch sets them up', 'World-class stuff'; 'Allchurcharama'; and 'Golden boy blinder'. And all this is reporting on a match in which, at the end of forty-five minutes, the Manchester men were leading by four goals to one.

One journalist reported: 'Alex James, Charles Buchan, and David Jack were never better than Ivor Allchurch, George Eastham and Albert Quixall were yesterday.' And of these three, Ivor stood out. As the *Sunday Express* put it: 'Allchurch was a great form in the World Cup, but even there I never saw him as outstanding as this.' A writer named Ken Waite added another dimension to the many Allchurch eulogies which were penned that day, when he wrote:

'Soccer's nearest approach to perpetual motion, Wilf McGuiness, ran out of puff on Saturday. At the end of this 90 minute chase-me-Charlie, he staggered over to Ivor Allchurch and gripped his hand. It was the first time he'd been able to strike up an acquaintance during the whole match . . . Newcastle's golden boy, surely the most beautiful mover in the game, played McGuiness like an angler plays a trout . . . I waited to congratulate Ivor Allchurch after the match. But he side-stepped me at the players' entrance. Then I really knew how Wilf McGuiness felt!'

When Ivor took stock following the final game of his first season at

Gallowgate, he felt reasonably pleased with life. Everyone agreed that he had made a striking contribution to the Newcastle United cause; he had struck up many worthwhile friendships inside and outside football (he and Bob Stokoe, in particular, were close); whilst it would have been wrong to say that Esme was not missing her family, she, Ivor and young John had settled, quickly, in the Kenton district of Newcastle; and Ivor was particularly pleased with the warm reaction of the Geordie fans. All in all, life was very good for the family Allchurch, and they had little doubt that Ivor had made the right decision in signing for the 'Magpies'. The Geordies, they felt, were their kind of people.

## 1959-60

On returning for pre-season training, Ivor was disturbed to learn from the press that there was a possibility that Charlie Mitten might be going to leave the club to join Leeds United. What made the situation worse was that the factions on the Newcastle board held contrasting views as to whether or not to keep their manager. As it turned out, the differences were resolved, and Mitten remained at St. James's Park after signing a three-year contract.

Not surprisingly, Ivor was relieved. Everything else apart, Mitten had brought him to Newcastle and the pair had developed a mutual respect; a new manager might have had a different view of the men he wanted. He was relieved, too, to learn that Stan Seymour (the leader of one of the factions on the Newcastle board) had called for all parties to give their manager full support. Differences had to be forgotten; the successful future of Newcastle United was what mattered. Although the professionals at St. James's Park at that time were more concerned with footballing matters than with what happened in the club's boardroom, this news was well received. Now they could get on with playing football and with improving the club's performances in League and Cup.

Unfortunately, the 1959-60 campaign started with a comprehensive home defeat by Tottenham Hotspur. The London club, with Ivor's former Swansea team-mate, Cliff Jones, in dazzling form, scored five goals against Newcastle's one. There followed a dismal run of results which, by the end of October, saw the St. James's Park men adrift in eighteenth place in the division. Eight of the fifteen matches which the club had played had been lost. In response, Mitten rang the changes in his side, though Ivor was ever-present, and a revival started with a match against Everton. To the amazement of the home supporters, Newcastle won 8-2, and it was the deadly trio of Allchurch, White and Eastham which inflicted the damage upon the Merseysiders. Even though the following match was lost, thereafter the side put together a run of four wins in succession, which improved the confidence of both the team and its supporters.

That sequence started with a 3-1 victory, in the mud, over Blackburn Rovers which had the press drooling about Ivor's play. The *Newcastle Journal* reported that the victory was achieved: 'Thanks to Ivor Allchurch for a display of majestic dribbling through the Gallowgate mud. A display which will be recalled in years to come along with royal performances from "Shack" and Jackie.' And 'Allchurch dribbled forty yards diagonally from right half to wide on the left, finishing with a perfect back-heel which Scanlon hit towards the post . . . '

*The People* and the *Sunday Express* echoed the *Journal's* sentiment:

> 'Allchurch was outstanding and directed the Newcastle attack,' and' 'Allchurch was unstoppable – always busy, very often brilliant . . . I doubt whether the Welshman did his chances of getting a transfer much good! This game nailed once and for all the lie that he is too old . . . when the final whistle blew . . . Allchurch was still spry.'

It was the story behind the transfer request which also attracted much comment in Newcastle around that time. Ivor had requested permission to be released to play for Wales in a home international. The club had refused his request on the grounds that its position in the league did not warrant his being released to play for Wales. Since Ivor had made what he considered to be a straightforward agreement with manager Mitten that he would be released if selected by his country, it was little wonder that he was aggrieved. His request for a transfer was his response to what he saw as the club 'breaking its word'. Meantime, given his nature, he continued to give his all to the Newcastle cause, and, in due course, happily for all concerned, the controversy was put to rest.

During the period of this dispute Ivor continued to delight his admirers. For example, Frank Douglas, reporting on a superb New-castle victory at Bolton, praised the Magpies' strike trio and gave Ivor a full 10 points as his assessment of the Welshman's performance. He reported that, 'Allchurch had his greatest game since he moved from Swansea to Newcastle', which, given the quality of many of Ivor's performances for the Geordie club, was praise indeed. In addition. He had been in outstanding form in many other matches around that time, including during a 4-1 victory over Arsenal and a 4-3 win at Maine Road against a fine Manchester City side. Yet, the victory at Bolton was special. The team as a whole seemed to acquire a collec-tive sixth sense which enabled its members to respond to and provoke each other's play in order to achieve a level of superlative performance rarely seen on a football field. After the match, a delighted Mitten claimed that his side had 'played more like Barcelona than any British team'.

Although the team was not able to sustain this level of performance, when the season ended it found itself in eighth position in the First Division. This was no more than a modest improvement on the club's position at the end of the previous campaign, but it was significantly better than the situation at the end of October when it languished in Eighteenth place. Surely, the Geordie fans mused, they would see the benefit of this improvement during the 1960-1 campaign.

As far as Ivor was concerned, he could look back on another full and successful season of football. He had played in all but one of the Newcastle club's games and, together with White, Eastham, Hughes, McMichael, Scoular, Stokoe, Bell and Harvey, he had formed the nucleus of a side which had matured during what had began as a difficult season. He felt reasonably confident about the season ahead, but, like the majority of people at St. James's Park, he did not have the slightest inkling of the problems which were to face the club during what turned out to be one of the most traumatic periods in its history.

## 1960-1

The news that George Eastham wished to be transferred; that the club had refused his request; and that the player had absented himself from St. James's Park, dominated pre-season discussion on Tyneside. The player insisted that it was his intention to challenge the club's right to retain him against his will, and that he was going to enlist the support of the P.F.A. in his fight. As it happened, Ivor also put in a request for a transfer on the same day as had Eastham, though Allchurch's case and approach were quite different. Ivor's request concerned Esme's wish to go back to Wales. Despite the fact that the family had settled so well in Newcastle, she had discovered that she was pregnant, and, after losing the last baby she had carried, she felt that she needed to be near her family during the confinement. Doctors had assured her that all was well, but, naturally, the psychological pressures involved were considerable. From Ivor's point of view, Esme's concerns had to take first place in the matter, hence his request to leave.

Even though his request was refused, Ivor continued to serve the club in the only way he knew – by giving a hundred per cent every time he wore the Newcastle jersey. But he had another problem, too. Whilst the team won its first two games of the season, by the end of October, the Magpies' had lost eight of the fifteen matches played. Mitten's response was to shuffle his pack in search of the successful blend he had believed he had discovered during the previous campaign.

One of his ideas was to play Ivor at centre-forward; but the Welsh-man was adamant that he was not a number nine. He was convinced that, in Len White, Newcastle already had a quality leader of the attack, and that for his own part he was an inside-forward. Mitten, however, persisted, so much so that Ivor refused to appear in the number nine shirt on three occasions. News of this behaviour – so completely out-of-character with the name Allchurch – reached the press, and, when cornered by a *Daily Mirror* journalist, Ivor was reported as 'grimly repeating' that he did not want to play in Len White's position. Two events conspired to change Ivor's attitude. First, Charlie Mitten backed down; and second, about the same time, the club's doctor and a specialist gynaecologist were able to reassure Esme that, with hospital care, all would be well with her pregnancy. At this Ivor withdrew his transfer request, and, whilst there were complications, David, a baby brother for the first Allchurch son, John, was born in the March of 1961. The parents were delighted, although Ivor did joke about the lad being eligible to play for England.

By then, however, the team was struggling in the lower regions of the first division. The 'Barcelona combination' of the previous season was but a memory, and, despite winning the last two matches of the season, scoring eight goals in the process, United ended the campaign in twenty-first place and were relegated. For the first time since 1947, the Gallowgate faithful had to face up to second-division football.

Nevertheless, as they did so, they could look back on another campaign in which the name 'Allchurch' had been inscribed with skill and endeavour on the annals of Newcastle United Football club. During the season, only Duncan Neale had played in more matches than Ivor, who was, again, second top scorer for the club. Furthermore, despite the club's lack of success, the quality of Allchurch's performances were often emphasised by the press.

In September, for example, the *Sunday Express* in reporting a game at Nottingham Forest stated:

'Within . . . six minutes Allchurch got the ball in midfield, directed his attackers into position while the Nottingham defence stood apparently stupefied – and suddenly the ball was in the net.'

In the same month, it was West Bromwich Albion's turn to be mesmerised as the 'magpies' staged a 'come-back':

*The People* headline read 'Allchurch zips United home', and its report of the match included the sentence:

'By then the agile Allchurch took on West Bromwich single-handed, pouring out vintage magic as West Brom moved back back, back.'

The *Newcastle Journal's* report of the same game informed its readers that Ivor was 'The perfect footballer. He was terrific in all he attempted.' Since he was approaching his thirty-second birthday at the time, the vintage of the Allchurch wine, as noted in the *People* report, was clearly of prime quality.

When the side was defeated at Blackpool in a match which it should have won, one journalist, clearly influenced by Russian cosmonauts, wrote:

'Newcastle WERE the better team – if only because of the cosmic brilliance of Ivor Allchurch . . . He stood out Gagarin-high above everyone else on the field . . . no one could compare with Allchurch – not even Stanley Matthews.'

Many reports during that arduous campaign emphasised, not only Ivor's footballing qualities, but his endeavour. And this was reflected

*'Captain Ivor'.*

in the fact that, in the absence of Jimmy Scoular, the Welshman's team-mates were unanimous in electing him as captain, 'for a match against Fulham and until further notice'. Ivor's friend Bob Stokoe, who had been acting as captain, stood aside to allow him to take on this role and, as Bob said at the time, 'there's no one better equipped for the job'.

Other praise in the press for Ivor included comments in a report on a dour match against Nottingham Forest, when *The People*, referring to the Welshman, gave the opinion that:

'Throughout the match he lay back and snapped up anything loose to juggle and scheme – an artist among a crowd of artisans. It was Allchurch's cleverness . . . which provided the rare distinctive touches in this undistinguished game.'

Then, an *Evening Chronicle* report of a match with Blackburn Rovers, carried the headline: 'Allchurch Superb!' And that account carried the paragraph:

'Allchurch brought the house down as he veered to the left to stage a brilliant solo effort. He beat Dobing, Douglas, McEvoy and Taylor, then sent over a centre which flashed in front of Leyland. Allchurch was outstanding!'

Given that he was playing in what was an unsuccessful side, these and many other reports were indicative not only of the quality of his football, but of his dedicated efforts to support the Newcastle cause. Little wonder then that, when the 'Ivor wants to go back to Wales' rumours started to re-appear, all kinds of suggestions were made with a view to persuading him to stay at St. James's Park. Whilst, of course, it was impractical, the one which touched him even more than the pleading letters from fans, was the idea suggested by a Newcastle journalist that he could live and train in Wales whilst playing for United.

*1961-2*

As Division Two beckoned and the Allchurch-is-going tales began to proliferate, Ivor found himself elected club captain again. Mitten said that he had been impressed with the player's dedication to the task during the previous season and felt that Ivor was the natural choice to lead the club. Meantime, the *Evening Chronicle* was campaigning to make sure that the Welshman stayed at Gallowgate, and in Mitten they found a willing ally. He told the paper:

'I am not at all resigned to the prospect of losing Ivor All-church. With the maximum wage restriction removed we can afford to pay Allchurch in relation to his value to United, which is tremendous! . . . Tell me where and at what cost we can replace him?'

However, Mitten, himself was also the subject of a great deal of gossip. Indeed, the bulk of the press was convinced that, after taking Newcastle into the Second Division his days were numbered at St. James's Park. Yet, to the surprise of many, when the new season opened, Mitten was still at the Gallowgate helm.

As far as Ivor was concerned, following the abolition of the maximum wage arrangements, he found himself to be earning the princely sum of £60.00 per week. This helped matters in the Allchurch household, and with Esme expecting another baby, the increase was very welcome. At St. James's Park, however, Ivor found that he was now part of a club which, to use the metaphor of friendly apologists was 'in transition'. Bob Stokoe and Jimmy Scoular had gone, George Eastham was, still, in dispute with the club, and, in due course, Len White was allowed to leave for Huddersfield.

During that lack-lustre Second Division season, only Dick Keith, Alf McMichael and Ivor himself of the outfield players appeared in English League matches on more than thirty occasions. Ivor was top scorer with eleven goals, and missed only two League matches – one of those because he was playing for Wales against England at Cardiff, his forty-sixth 'cap' for his country. That was his sixth 'cap' in succession following his recall to the Welsh side, and he was extremely keen to add to the number which had been awarded to him. Playing for Wales was always a tremendous privilege as far as Ivor was concerned, which was why, when the Welsh team was announced, he was angered by Newcastle's initial refusal to release him. Ivor protested and, when the club reluctantly agreed to let him play for Wales, he felt moved to resign the club captaincy. It was the second time during his career at St. James's Park that he had been confronted with an obdurate attitude on the part of the club in its refusal to allow him to play for his country.

Later in October, after Sheffield United had won a League Cup replay at Newcastle, Charlie Mitten was sacked. With Alderman McKeag (who was abroad at the time) complaining that he had not been consulted, Ivor found that the two men who had been instrumental in signing him were no longer influential. This hardly helped Ivor's state of mind, and matters were exacerbated in December when Esme gave birth, prematurely, to a little girl who lived just two days. Subsequently, complications set in and Esme had to spend three months in hospital.

In Esme's absence, Ivor found himself faced with the problem of looking after the two children whilst continuing to play. Clearly, this was extremely difficult, and Esme's sister, Betty (who was married to Ivor's younger brother), immediately took the baby to Yorkshire – where Len was playing for Sheffield United – and looked after him there. Meantime, Ivor, with tremendous support from neighbours had to look after young John, see Esme as often as he could, and carry on with his footballing. Not surprisingly, it was a far from easy time, and, despite the willing support which he received Ivor badly missed the loving care of his wider family. In many respects that period was the 'last straw' as far as the 'Golden Boy' was concerned, and he determined then that he would leave St. James's Park at the end of the season. Cardiff City were said to be interested in signing him, and, if matters developed, he was of a mind to go there.

Nevertheless, throughout these months, and until the final whistle sounded at the end of the campaign, Ivor continued to delight his admirers by giving himself heart and soul to the Newcastle cause. As ever, the match reports and press comment reflected the Allchurch genius, his demeanour and his attitude.

The *Evening Chronicle*, reporting on two friendlies with Sunderland, let it be known that the Wearsiders 'had no one to open up play as did Ivor Allchurch', and 'Allchurch made the efforts of the Sunderland schemers look pedestrian'. In reporting on a defeat at Southampton, the paper argued that 'Newcastle's captain, Allchurch, put on a terrific show. He was immaculate in everything he did, the complete inside-forward; one of the masters. Then, when Newcastle lost at Anfield, Frank McGee, referring to the Newcastle club's refusal to release Ivor to play for Wales, wrote:

> 'Talent like this deserves to be shown against the background of International football, deserves it as a right, not a grudging favour. At Anfield, Allchurch was the brain and heart of the Newcastle team which gave Liverpool . . . a fright. He did enough on his own to make this result a mockery. His subtle variations of pace baffled Liverpool . . . His equally skilful control of shooting power . . . had Liverpool's fabulous record . . . trembling.'

And there were many more tributes of this kind, but none more pertinent, perhaps, than Vince Wilson's homily about the man Allchurch. Wilson wrote:

'For me . . . Ivor Allchurch is the North East's MAN OF THE YEAR. He has shown:

COURAGE    There has not been a harder fighter in Newcastle's struggle.

GUTS    Though not the happiest man on the St. James's Park staff he never shirked.

LOYALTY    George Eastham . . . left Newcastle snookered, Allchurch showed tolerance, understanding and loyalty.

The quiet-speaking Welshman could have been pulled many a flanker to further his ends. But typical of Allchurch, he once told me: 'I couldn't walk into a football field without giving anything less than my best . . .'

Newcastle trainer, Norman Smith . . . told me: 'I've never known any player quite like Ivor. He's had every reason to be nasty – but he's pulled out his guts for Newcastle United.'

And these comments are but indicative of the many which appeared in the press during that period. Not only was Ivor seen to be a player of special talent, he was also regarded as a wonderful clubman. No wonder he was loved – no other word will suffice – by the Gallowgate faithful who had begun to take the tall Welshman to their collective heart on that October day in 1958, and had seen their admiration blossom into a special relationship the quality of which very few footballers have engendered with their fans.

Sadly for those Newcastle supporters, they were to lose their hero during the 1962 close-season. Like their Swansea counterparts, they were very sad to see him go. Yet they wished him well, and comforted themselves with heart-warming memories of his many outstanding performances in the black and white shirt of Newcastle United.

Perhaps Bob Stokoe's words best draw down the curtain on Ivor's sojourn at St. James's Park: 'Ivor was just a lovely man, and a lovely player . . . who simply glided past people . . . I reckon that the 1951 team was the best I ever saw and Ivor would have graced that!'

Wor Ivor! Wor Ivor, indeed!!

# CHAPTER EIGHT

# *A Bluebird*

Was Cardiff City a big club? That was very much the issue that was debated and had to be decided when Ivor signed for Cardiff City in August 1962. The City had just been relegated from Division One, a fate they had also suffered as recently as 1957. Their fans had relished the two periods at the top level 1952-7, and 1960-2 and had taken them as an indication of the club's true status as *the* big team in Wales. Ninian Park was an impressive place in those days and players such as Nat Lofthouse and Ivor Allchurch spoke of how much they enjoyed playing there in big games. The biggest games, of course, were the international matches against England when 60,000 would be packed into the ground, but Cardiff City themselves could be a major attraction. Almost 55,000 had watched their vital promotion game against Aston Villa in April 1960, and eleven months later 47,000 turned up to see City beat a Spurs side that was on its way to winning The Double. City fans longed for big games of that sort, longed for Ninian Park to be one of the important venues in British football.

But how was this to be achieved? In 1962 City fans were far from convinced that the board were developing the team in the right way. There was particular disquiet at what was taken as a tendency to rely on fading Welsh stars. The 30-year-old Trevor Ford had joined Cardiff in 1953 but, after initial success things had turned rather sour and by the time of his last games in 1957, fans were embarrassed to see him playing out of position on the wing and by his disputes with the management. Then early in 1962, as the City slid down the table, they signed Mel Charles from Arsenal, a player with a big name and undoubted talent but with a distinct tendency to injury. Now there was the 32-year-old Ivor as well and perhaps not surprisingly there were mutterings on the terrace. Things were to come to a head a year later when the 31-year-old John Charles was signed from Roma. At that point the journalist Gareth Bowen contributed a sharp piece to the *South Wales Echo* condemning the whole saga and referring as he did so to the phenomenon of 'the dying Swan', the place of origin of these stars of yesteryear having been duly noted in the Canton stand. More positively, Bowen argued that what the club really needed was a policy of bringing to excellence its own youngsters. Quite rightly he pointed out that the two players who had most thrilled the Ninian Park faithful in recent years were Gerry Hitchins and Graham Moore. Hitchens, whom Bowen described as running around Ninian Park like 'a young colt in a new field' had been sold to Aston Villa whilst Moore, likened by Brian Glanville to the great Raymond Kopa, had moved on to Chelsea. It seemed to be young stars out, old men in. Was this the way back to division One? This is the context in which Ivor became a Bluebird. There were many imponderables. Did he point the way forward? Would he be a 'dying Swan'? Would his class win him a new set of fans? Anticipation mixed with apprehension as Ivor drove into Sloper Road.

The local press, of course, was full of the Ivor story. Throughout the summer there was speculation as to whether City's two-year quest for the Newcastle player would be successful. Would the Newcastle board accept the offer? And would Ivor be able to clear last minute difficulties over accrued benefits and his cut of the transfer fee? It was understood that the player was prepared to take a wages cut to come to Cardiff (from £60 to £40 per week) but there was an understanding that eventually there would be a job for him on the staff at Ninian Park. But several concerns remained. On the Saturday before the season started, Ivor appeared in a blue shirt as he captained the Cardiff team in what was described as the usual 'half-baked' trial. For Peter Corrigan Ivor's performance was 'languid but promising' and was climaxed by a late run with a shot going in from an impossible angle. The judgement was that he had 'taken the wind out of the critics' but nevertheless when Ivor went to his car at the end of the match to start his journey home to Swansea he found that, for some reason or other, his tyres had been let down.

The opening game of the season was to be a week later at home against, irony of ironies, Newcastle United. It was made absolutely clear that this was a game that 'City must win'. The Magpies would be tough opponents and all eyes would be on Dave Hilley the inside-forward signed from Third Lanark as a replacement for Ivor at a fee about twice the £18,000 that City paid Newcastle. Before the game Bill Jones, City's manager since 1958, gave his players a pep talk in which he made it clear why they needed to win; there would be a £9 bonus if victory ensured a place in the top six, success was essential if 'relegation blues' were to be swept aside and big crowds attracted, and above all a good start was essential for Ivor's sake as 'already the critics were lying in wait to hammer the latest city signing'.

On a glorious August afternoon over 27,000 fans turned up to see what Ivor and the City could do. What the crowd were given was first class entertainment, for the match finished 4-4, a very different scenario from the grim relegation struggles of a few months earlier. The crowd had been given their money's worth but there were no illusions. The weaknesses were apparent; four goals had been conceded at home and at half time the City had been 1-3 down. And yet, as Jim Hill consoled his readers, it's 'not a bad side' that 'gives goals away and pulls it back from 1-3'. There were heroes that day. Barrie Hole, Swansea-born but a City player since his youth, had reassured the crowd as he ran out, for many had thought that this 'brilliant' mid-field player would have moved on during the summer. But more was to come for that afternoon the attacking half-back scored twice.

Even more impressive was Cardiff's new left-winger Peter Hooper who had joined from Bristol Rovers for a £7,000 fee. The Ninian Park faithful had always loved wingers and as Hooper drove in City's opening goal with his left foot there was an instant recognition for a new hero. The afternoon as a whole had been a case of a 'groggy defence' at one end and plenty of goals at the other. But what of the team effort generally? It was in this respect that Ivor had triumphed. For him it was a 'double success' as Peter Corrigan explained: as a player he had both dropped back to give 'his troubled defenders an escape route' and moved forward to inspire attacks and as a captain it was he would inspired the vital second-half rally. For Jim Hill, Ivor was 'immaculate'.

Many of us who were there on that August afternoon shared Corrigan's surprise at what we thought of as a new Ivor. Perhaps we all subscribed to a somewhat stereotypical view of a player we still tended to envisage in Swansea colours. We knew of his sublime passing skills and of his two-footed shooting power but we had not thought of him particularly as a fighter and leader. The revaluation was to continue four days later at Norwich. At the end of a scoreless game Ivor came off 'angry and dejected'; as the referee had not allowed a goal he had 'scored' from a 30 yard indirect free-kick; the keeper had handled the ball but it was adjudged to be already over the line. It had been a frus-

*'Left foot "screamer" en route'.*

trating if exciting game but again it was one in which Ivor had excelled. When defender Trevor Peck had left the field Ivor dropped back to left-half, but in truth, as Peter Corrigan saw it, he was 'everywhere'. *The South Wales Echo's* correspondent was totally won over. 'Through it all,' he reported back to Cardiff, 'strolled Allchurch, a complete footballer, a giant of a captain.' Three days later City won 2-1 at Derby with Ivor scoring the winner. This was City's first away win for ten months. Once more it was 'the fighting spirit' which had inspired, a spirit that had been sadly lacking earlier in the year when it had been so badly needed. It was Ivor who was credited with inspiring this new attitude. 'Surely,' argued the *'Echo'*, 'he is one of the best skippers the club has ever had.'

The 'new' Ivor, however, could not disguise more general weaknesses. The City now lost four games in a row including home matches against Norwich and Middlesborough and consequently the directors panicked and did something they had never done before; they sacked their manager. Following a 2-1 defeat at the Vetch in which Peter Davies and Roy Saunders had bottled up Ivor after his brilliant first half, manager Bill Jones and coach and former star Wilf Grant were asked to pack their bags. Both men had many friends in the Cardiff area and the dramatic dismissals left a nasty taste. Some diversion was badly needed and again Ivor was on hand. He was 'magnificent' in a 5-2 home victory over the Swans and was now being referred to as one of three people constituting 'a shadow management', the others being veterans Ernie Curtis and Ron Stitfall. In fact the managerless club was now enjoying something of a goal glut, scoring six at Preston in late September. A month later on a grey day only 12,000 turned up to see City play against Scunthorpe, but they won 4-0 and Ivor who scored twice was outstanding. It was very apparent now for the small group of reporters who had to cover every Cardiff game, that it was Ivor alone who made their jobs worthwhile. Who else could make a late October game against Scunthorpe memorable? 'Call it Ivor's game,' wrote Peter Corrigan, for 'Ivor's class stood out like a beacon.'

*Charles J., Charles M., Allchurch I. v. Middlesborough, 12.9.64.*

By scoring two and making two he had 'proved himself the most valuable player City had possessed in a long long time'. Tudor James thought that this had been 'the greatest game of his life', whilst Lloyd Lewis reported that Ivor had 'revealed his true genius'. All three reporters waxed eloquently about his second goal, 'the best goal of his long career'. Corrigan recalled how he had 'swayed and soft-shoed like Gene Kelly past three defenders', before 'cracking the ball' into the net. Lloyd Lewis described how a Scunthorpe defender was 'struck still' by Ivor's flicking the ball from foot to foot, 'for a second nothing happened as though Allchurch was waiting for a cry of Olé, then he hammered home the goal'. Modestly Ivor explained how 'sometimes everything clicks into place. I don't think I've ever played better'.

Meanwhile the fans waited to see who the new manager would be. Of course they wanted a big name, they wanted an assurance that the board had real ambitions. Two former Wales greats, Alf Sherwood and Tommy Jones were amongst the early favourites but in November it was George Swindin, who had managed Arsenal for four years before moving only earlier that year to Norwich, who was appointed. Certainly this was a big name and the way in which the Cardiff directors were prepared to pay more than Norwich suggested somewhat ruthless determination. Furthermore, Mel Charles who had played with Swindin at Arsenal was able to report that the new boss, who after all had been for many years a great Arsenal goalkeeper, was very much a 'real players' manager'. Clearly Cardiff were fighting hard to stay big. But out on the pitch it was not easy. It was indeed a tough division, 'the hardest of all to get out of' as Swindin was quick to point out. It was not easy to live with the leading clubs. None of us who were there will ever forget the November game against Stoke when we looked through the gloom at Stanley Matthews, the 50-year-old right-winger. 'At least we've never signed anyone that old,' joked a wag at the Grangetown end, but City could only draw 1-1. What Cardiff were up against was made clear on trips to the north-east. On December 1 over 37,000 cheered Sunderland to a 2-1 win at Roker Park as the home team hung on to a thirty-game undefeated home run. City played well, a favourite opponent Stan Anderson praised their efforts, but there had been little push up front. Hooper missed a penalty and inside-forwards Durban and Allchurch were 'faulty with the final pass'. Two weeks later City were at St. James's Park where in front of over 27,000 they lost through two late goals. Graham Vearncombe

*Ivor heading for goal v. Newcastle, 1962.*

was great in goal but the man who impressed the knowledgeable crowd was their former hero Ivor Allchurch who was man-marked by Iley to no avail. Local reporter Maurice Smith concluded that 'There was no player in the Newcastle side who could match Allchurch in footwork and the ability to dictate the game'. His 'trickery' led to a Hooper goal and then as Newcastle went all out for an equaliser it was he would had 'master-minded a packed defence'. In short 'there had been no checking Allchurch' who had 'threatened to send all Newcastle away red-faced'.

Nonetheless, Cardiff were losing as many games as they won and consequently it was not going to be a season of glory. Ivor had more than answered all the early critics, but the team was clearly destined for mid-table and in the end finished in tenth place. For the history books it will always be Peter Hooper's season. It was his only campaign at Ninian Park for in the summer he was sold to Bristol City leaving the fans with memories of his astonishing left foot shot and the 22 goals he scored in 40 games. He was an exciting winger but, as City historian John Crooks points out, we should remember how many of his goals were 'set up by Allchurch who himself scored 12 in 35 games'. As he had breathed new life into Hooper's career, Ivor had also brought on his fellow inside-forward Alan Durban who now moved on to greater things at Derby County.

With Hooper, Durban and several other players gone there was an urgent need for replacements but in fact John Charles was the only significant summer signing. 'Can you work the miracle?' was what a somewhat 'cynical' Gareth Bowen asked in the open-letter to which reference has already been made. Cynicism became more general when it was learned that the manager George Swindin had been opposed to the signing of Charles. There seemed to be an element of clutching at straws as Cardiff attempted to escape from Second Division anonymity. Just over 22,000 turned up to see 'Big John' make his début. For some that was a disappointing figure, it was fewer than for Ivor's début a year earlier but how much smaller it would have been but for the new centre-forward. Charles certainly gave them all something to remember as he scored a goal with a 75-yard free kick, but Ivor scored a goal too and that was to be something of an appetiser for overall it was to be very much Ivor's season.

The team did poorly, winning only fourteen League games, finishing fifteenth and once again having to sack a manager. Swindin's team had been ravaged by injuries but the fans and perhaps the players too never really took to a man who always gave the impression that he was still at Arsenal. In the midst of mediocrity Ivor got on with the job and throughout exuded sheer professionalism leavened with brilliance. Remarkably he played in 41 League games missing only a Christmas holiday match at Preston and was top scorer with twelve goals.

In late September 1963 there were over 37,000 at Roker Park, the ground where Ivor had made his international début thirteen years earlier, to see one of the greatest scoring feats ever witnessed at that

*Cardiff City, 1963-4.*
*Back row: D. Murray, R. Stitfall, J. Charles, D. John, G. Vearncombe, M. Charles, T. Edwards, B. Hole.*
*Middle row: P. King, D. Scott, I. Allchurch, A. McIntosh. Front row: D. Tapscott, C. Baker.*

famous venue. In a thrilling game in which City, with only eight fit men towards the end, did well to get a point in a 3-3 draw with a team which was lying second in the table. What the crowd would remember most was a brilliant Allchurch hat-trick all of which took place in a sixteen minute burst which started in the sixth minute. For his first, Ivor beat two men on the half-way line before running thirty yards and firing in a fierce shot from outside the box; his second saw him swivel on the edge of the box before sending in a left foot drive which cannoned off the far post into the goal; and the third came after he carved his way in from the right before scoring with a shot from twenty yards out which 'screamed' inside the near post. Peter Corrigan described it as 'the most fantastic hat-trick' that he had ever seen. Obviously Allchurch was the 'Man of the match' and he was cheered off by the Roker crowd. To read the reports of this game is to catch all the terrific atmosphere of football in the north-east, where huge crowds above all wanted to be pleased by football artists like Ivor Allchurch. It is to be reminded too of how those of us who watched football being played in the old Second Division would look every year to see whether there would be games against Sunderland, Newcastle and Middlesborough; all too often these fixtures would be the only guarantee of seeing real ball-players and exciting games.

Ivor was back in the north-east in the November and this time over 38,000 paid to see him thrill his old fans at St. James' Park. This time Newcastle had brought in Stan Anderson from Sunderland just to mark him, but according to Vince Wilson: 'The Welsh Wizard shrugged off Anderson, the crowd and the rest', as he prompted his side into giving the home team a 4-0 'roasting'. The bitterest pill for the Geordie crowd was that Ivor scored a 'brilliant goal'. In the 55th minute he rounded a defender and sent in a 'low sizzling shot' which beat Hollins in goal and which brought the crowd to its feet to give their former hero 'a tremendous ovation'. He also had a hand in two other goals and, noting that, Wilson made an observation which very neatly summed-up Ivor's general role at that time. 'But Allchurch,' wrote Wilson, 'covering tremendous ground was still the top brain behind the slick Cardiff attack.'

Slick attack notwithstanding, Cardiff were just a run-of-the-mill team and the sacking of Swindin more than anything else just revealed general frustration. For all his own professional commitment, Ivor, like his many fans, was now fully aware that there were going to be no miracles worked at Ninian Park. In June 1964 he must have been aware that his satisfaction in playing for Cardiff was not going to increase, for the newly appointed manager was his old adversary Jimmy Scoular. There was nothing that Ivor did not know about a man with whom he had played at Newcastle. Perhaps the very nature of British football is that it requires its Scoulars and its Ivors. The *Times* obituary of Scoular who died in 1998 stressed that the former Portsmouth and Newcastle wing-half was 'one of the finest long-range passers of his day', but conceded that he was better known for his determination which 'occasionally stretched beyond the limits of fair play' and for being 'a muscular and vocal giant'. He had been a fierce tackler, an inspiring captain and a player who was guaranteed to make 'errant colleagues suffer the considerable force of his tongue'. If Ivor had not particularly enjoyed being a team-mate or opponent of this short balding feisty Scot, even less was he going to relish playing for him.

Scoular's first season at Ninian Park was not surprisingly Ivor's last, but once again Ivor was the club's top scorer with 15 goals from only 27 appearances. In October he picked up a thigh-strain which led to his missing a couple of games, but when he was fit again he found himself playing in the reserves. In fact Ivor was out of the first team between mid-October and the middle of February during which time it became known that he wanted to leave the club. Having started the season by going twelve games without a win Scoular had decided to opt for youth and pace and in Ivor's place he played the young Peter King who was in the process of being converted from a winger. Without Ivor, however, the side slipped into the bottom quarter of the table and clearly Scoular had to swallow his pride and bring Ivor back. Back he came to score nine vital goals, goals which eventually ensured a final position of thirteenth in the table. The first goal after his return, and it was the 200th of his career, came at Southampton where his overall performance was described as 'scintillating'. Highly placed Southampton expected to win this game but the crowd found themselves 'frequently applauding' Ivor's 'vintage' display. Ken Wimshurst declared that he was glad that he 'didn't have to mark Allchurch every week'. The highlight of Ivor's season and what a bitter-sweet moment it must have been, came in the April game that season against Swansea Town at Ninian Park. A crowd of 16,000 saw the City beat the Swans and in so doing virtually condemn them to the Third Division. Three Swansea boys, Hole, Allchurch and John Charles were wearing blue that day and they were responsible for all the goals. Charles scored twice and Ivor hit a hat-trick. Tom Lyons described 'the heroes ovation' that the inside-forward was given. The highlight of the afternoon came with his second goal; on the edge of the box he floated past Peter Davies and then released a shot with the outside of his right foot which curled inside the far post.

The City might have sealed the fate of the Swans but Jimmy Scoular, a born worrier, was still not confident about his own team's prospects. He warned that they were 'not out of the wood' and 'that there was no room for complacency'. He made it clear that he would continue to ring the changes in his line-up. More and more it was to the younger players that he was looking and as City completed an Easter double over Coventry, with Ivor scoring twice in the home game, it was players like Don Murray, Bernard Lewis and George Johnston who were catching the eye. When John Crooks later spoke to Murray about that season the centre-half recalled what a pleasure and privilege it was for youngster like himself to play alongside the older stars. 'There was a saying among the players', he explained, 'if you are in trouble give it to Ivor.'

Scoular's dependence on youth had been very apparent in the club's European games. In the previous season under Swindin the City had won the Welsh Cup and now for the first time for the club the prize was a place in the European Cup Winners' Cup. A new chapter was opening for Cardiff City for from the outset it was obvious that the European road was paved with gold. League attendances were diminishing but obviously the masses relished the prospect of exciting two-legged cup-ties which at the same time confirmed the club's status as an international force. The fans felt back at the centre of things. In the 1964-5 season Sporting Lisbon attracted 25,000 to Ninian Park and Real Zaragoza did even better for 38,000 turned out for that quarter-final game. This exciting new venture, however, came just a little too late for Ivor. He played in City's initial European fixture against Esjberg of Denmark but thereafter was left out of the side. Allchurch admirers have no reason to think kindly of Jimmy Scoular but it should be noted that as a manager he took full advantage of the new European dispensation. He made winning the Welsh Cup a priority and he subsequently ensured that his players were fired-up for the big European encounters. In 1968 he took City to the semi-final, and in 1971 a crowd of 47,500 saw Real Madrid defeated at Ninian Park. That was the season the Bluebirds just missed out on promotion to Division One, eventually finishing third. Scoular was rough diamond but for a while and after a sticky start he made Cardiff City one of the strongest Second Division sides.

Meanwhile, Ivor had departed. He played his last game in a blue shirt on April 24 1965 when there were a mere 9,932 fans at Ninian Park to see him score the first goal in a 3-1 victory over Rotherham. With the new European dimension and with new stars emerging (John Toshack who was twenty years younger than Ivor was to make his début six months after that Rotherham match) there was always a danger that Ivor's three seasons at Cardiff playing in an ordinary mid-table side would be somewhat eclipsed. But that was not the case. The *cognoscenti* in the stands and on the terraces, and perhaps above all in the press-box were fully aware of how privileged they had been. They had expected the long passes and the fearsome shots, but they could never have envisaged either the completeness of Ivor's game or how breathtakingly brilliant some of goals would be. The delightful and delicate Swan had become a much more rounded player and there was widespread admiration for the way in which this man in his mid-thirties could so whole-heartedly commit himself to the rigours of long campaigns in a tough no-nonsense division and yet still display both vision and magic. Even on the bleakest nights we went to Ninian Park knowing that whatever happened we were guaranteed a glass or two of vintage Allchurch wine. There would be lots of huffing and puffing from the bit-players but at the core of the game there would be guaranteed quality. Above all what we saw at Cardiff in those years was a remarkable and perhaps even unique display of how one man can be both a touch-player, an artist and a fully committed professional accepting full responsibility for the wider team game.

Ivor Allchurch's wonderful contribution to the enjoyment of football at Ninian Park in the early 1960's has been justifiably noted by the club's historians. In Peter Jackson's 1974 history Ivor takes his place in mid-field in 'The Greatest City Eleven of All Time'. For John Crooks, whose various volumes have done so much to keep alive the great memories, Ivor was 'quite simply the best ball-playing, all-round footballer to have played for Cardiff City in the post-war years.'

CHAPTER NINE

# The World Stage

The case for Ivor Allchurch's greatness is clinched by the remarkable way he sustained his international career. For those followers of the game whose standards are purely domestic, for whom the Football League is everything, the high point of Ivor's career must be the three seasons between 1958 and 1961 when he played for Newcastle in the old First Division. Subsequent seasons in the Second Division with Newcastle and Cardiff, and then in the Third and Fourth with Swansea, would seem to indicate a progressive decline. In reality things were a little more complicated than that. Allchurch was a class player whose skills stood out in the lower divisions. Almost automatically and entirely naturally he remained in the Welsh team. International competition was thought to be the ideal arena for the kind of game he played. He was needed to score vital goals, to split open highly-regarded defences, to stabilise makeshift and experimental sides and increasingly to encourage and prompt untried youngsters. All these things he did for Wales in an international career that lasted until 1966, eight years after his World Cup appearances in Sweden and sixteen years after his first cap.

Inevitably he became a record breaker. There was always a dispute as to how many times the great Billy Meredith had turned out for Wales but in 1962 Ivor was adjudged to be the new record holder when he won his 50th Cap in the match against Scotland. His final total was 68 caps, a statistic familiar to Welsh fans for many years. Given the greatly increased number of international opportunities which now exist it was a record that was bound to go. In time Ivor was overtaken by that flamboyant if inconsistent full-back Joey Jones, then by the midfield workhorse Peter Nicholas and eventually, and more satisfactorily, by two greats, Ian Rush and Neville Southall. Somehow, though, it is the 68 that sticks in the mind. Even more remarkably he was to equal the scoring record set by his original international partner, Trevor Ford. Both these Swansea boys scored 23 times for Wales.

*Training at Roehampton.*

Trevor's strike-rate was far higher, his goals coming in only 38 games, but Ivor's total is outstanding given that he rarely played as an out-and-out striker and was consigned to extensive midfield duties. In time, of course, a new record was set by another striker, the goal-machine Ian Rush. As a leading Welsh goal-scorer Ivor lives on in the list in excellent company.

The records, however, are less remarkable than the quality. As an ageing international player called up from the lower divisions Ivor went on grabbing the headlines and almost inevitably picking up the 'man of the match' tag. He was earning these plaudits in a rapidly changing international football schedule. There remained the Home International Championship, a tournament that survived until 1984 and which involved annual matches against England, Scotland and Northern Ireland. The England and Scotland fixtures were always regarded as the toughest challenges and success was elusive. In the years between Sweden and retirement from the international scene Allchurch played in thirteen matches against either England or Scotland and tasted success only once, a victory against Scotland in Cardiff in 1964. Those home internationals were closely contested and demand-

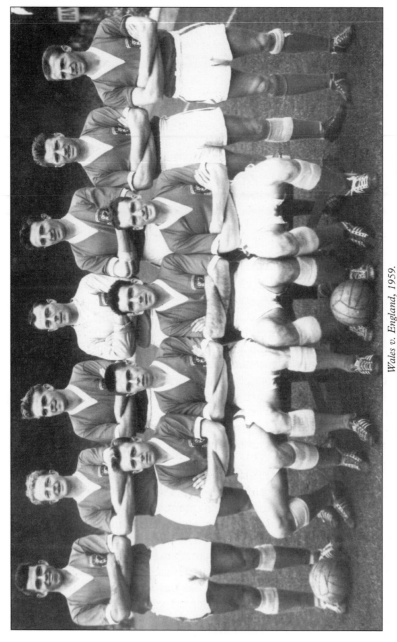

*Wales v. England, 1959.*

*Back row: Mel Nurse, Ivor, Graham Moore, Jack Kelsey, Mel Hopkins, Derek Sullivan, Cliff Jones.*
*Front row: Terry Medwin, Phil Woosnam, Stuart Williams, Vic Crowe.*

ing fixtures, and although Ivor was regularly picked out by reporters for his telling contributions there was little opportunity for Wales as a team to achieve glory. But now there were pastures new; for World Cup qualifications, a European Nations Championship and an increased number of friendlies with nations wanting experience against British opposition, took Wales to exotic locations and brought star teams to Cardiff. These new adventures had a little more romance and a welcome dimension of the unknown as compared to the traditional fixtures. The fans loved the notion of Wales as a potential world force, and the players enjoyed travelling to the world's great cities. Mel Nurse, one of Ivor's companions on several of these trips, has always maintained that one should never underestimate how much the footballers of that era, who lived quite modestly at home, enjoyed the privilege of staying the first-class hotels and generally being treated like VIPs. Certainly Ivor relished being on the world stage.

A new era for Welsh soccer began in 1961. Allchurch, having played for Wales regularly in the first two seasons after Sweden, was left out of the side for four games in 1960 which meant that he missed a 5-1 drubbing at Wembley. After what was an eighteen month absence he was recalled for the game against Northern Ireland in Belfast in April 1961. 'Ivor', announced Frank McGhee, 'is back with a bang'. Wales won 5-1, with their attack sparkling in the wet conditions. For Dennis Busher, Ivor was generally 'brilliant' and his goal came from 'a magnificent shot' after shaking off challengers. His return to the national team was timely, for two weeks later he was needed for the first leg of a one-off World Cup qualifying match against a highly thought-of Spanish team. There were 35,000 at Ninian Park to see Wales lose 2-1 to a visiting team that disappointed on the evening. On a rain-soaked pitch it was Wales who impressed, first by playing brilliantly for the opening twenty minutes and later by their 'never-say-die' attitude as they fought to save the game. The Spanish confessed that it was likely to be their most difficult match en-route to the World Cup finals in Chile and *ABC*, the Spanish daily paper, singled out Allchurch as having been the best Welsh player. Bill Paton spoke of how in that excellent opening phase Ivor had 'bewildered the Spanish defence with the pace and poise of his spectacular runs which had the crowd on its toes'. From 'one gem of a pass' Ken Leek should have scored, but later Allchurch worked a short corner with Medwin and from the cross Woosnam scored. In the later stages it was very much

*The Swansea contingent v. Spain, Cardiff 1961.*
*Terry Medwin, Graham Williams, Mel Nurse, Ivor.*

Ivor, together with Swansea Town's diminutive winger Graham 'Flicka' Williams, who inspired the Welsh challenge. It now seemed totally ridiculous that Allchurch had ever been left out of Welsh teams; Bill Paton spoke openly of selectors with 'red faces'.

Wales had been brave in that first leg but they had also, as Mel Charles confessed, 'been slightly over-awed'. Naturally there was some anxiety about the second leg. There would be a crowd in the region of 100,000 to see Spain play in their capital city, Madrid, where they had never lost to a British side. It was an evening when Alfredo di Stefano, the Argentinean centre-forward who now played for Spain and who was once described by Brian Glanville as 'perhaps the most complete footballer of all time', and Francisco 'Paco' Gento, the fastest and most admired of all wingers were expected to destroy the opposition. After the match there was rather less talk of the Spanish superstars and rather more about the men from 'Gales'. In drawing 1-1 Wales had fought all the way. In what he described as 'one of Wales's greatest performances' Roy Peskett picked out goalkeeper Kelsey and 'Flicka' Williams, who was playing his first game abroad, as heroes. There was praise too for Allchurch who was coolness itself throughout this passionate occasion. He delighted the crowd with a great goal: picking up a pass from Vic Crowe, and whilst on the run, he smashed a fierce surprise shot into the left-hand corner of the net. Minutes later he fired in another angled shot which beat the 'keeper but was cleared from the line (or from just over it according to some Welsh players) by defender Zoco. Di Stefano singled out Allchurch as 'the one world-class player' in the Welsh team. Subsequently there was speculation that Real Madrid were trying to sign him so as to keep him permanently in the massive stadium where, clearly, he had made such a big impact on that May evening in 1961.

Ten days later Wales played in Budapest where they lost 3-2 to a Hungarian side who were on their way to qualifying impressively for

*Training in Madrid, 1961.*
*(Ivor signed this photograph for Mel Nurse just before he died).*
*Back row: Mel Nurse, Mel Hopkins, Stuart Williams, Mel Charles, Graham Moore,*
*Ken Leek, Graham Williams, Cliff Jones, Jimmy Murphy, Ivor.*
*Front row: Jack Jones, Jack Kelsey, Phil Woosnam, Colin Baker.*

*131*

the World Cup Finals and who would eventually get through to the quarter-finals in Chile the following summer. Wales were 2-0 down after only six minutes and then, having fought back to 2-2, were unlucky to lose to a penalty scored by their old friend Tichy just seven minutes from the end. Kelsey was again a hero as was winger Cliff Jones. Allchurch was adjudged to be the visitors' 'most effective forward': he had been 'a constant danger' and it was his shot from the edge of the box that had at one stage levelled the scores. Socially it was a joyous visit and for years thereafter Mel Nurse would josh Ivor about how he had needed assistance to make his way back to the hotel after an Embassy reception. Few doubted that 'Pancho' Nurse had been tampering with Ivor's drinks.

Come the autumn and once again it was time to pay England at Cardiff. In 1961 the game finished 1-1 as it had done in 1959. Wales did not play well and perhaps the most interesting feature of the day was the record crowd of over 61,000, many of whom came to see 'the prodigal son' home from Italy; it was John Charles's first game in a red shirt for two years. Something of the sheer frustration that attended Welsh efforts in those Home Internationals can be gathered from that day's programme notes. The pen portrait of Allchurch spoke of how 'every Welsh supporter will be delighted that he was playing today': for many season, it was explained, 'he has been a great player and is still capable of winning a big game off his own bat'. The profile went on to say that 'he has strangely enough failed on a number of occasions to reproduce his best form in internationals' before, rather patronisingly, concluding that Allchurch 'is, notwithstanding, fully worthy of his place today'. That was a sour note to strike in a big-match programme and, revealingly, within a year it had been amended. When Scotland came to Ninian Park in October 1962 the same opening comments on Ivor winning games 'off his own bat' were followed not by a stricture but rather by the observation that 'since joining Cardiff City he has played some brilliant football'.

Earlier that year Wales had played friendly games in South America against two nations warming up for the World Cup finals to be held in Chile. First they played two games against the highly fancied Brazil who were indeed to be crowned world champions just one month later. For openers Wales, who had so impressed the Brazilians four years earlier, were entertained in the Maracana in Rio, that 'giant tureen of a stadium' to which a crowd of about 100,000 were attracted.

Wales had John Charles at centre-half playing in defiance of doctor's orders but he and the young Terry Hennessey could do little to check the 'elegant, unhurried, chess-game pace' of the Brazilians for whom Pelé and Garrincha were outstanding. Wales lost 3-1, with Pelé, who now seemed to Jimmy Murphy to be 'the complete master', scoring one goal and laying one on for Garrincha. Wales impressed briefly when Pelé was off but in general only 'played as well as allowed'. Inevitably, however, Ivor stood out for he was 'the ace schemer', and furthermore early in the second half he ran onto a long pass from Vic Crowe and as the ball passed him he smashed it into the net. This 'wondrous' goal was welcomed as evidence that Europeans had 'not surrendered everything best to the Latins'.

Four days later the two teams met again, this time in the huge sprawl of Sao Paolo, a city, it was noted, with a population far in excess of Wales. This was a game that Mike England, who came into the side in the place of Crowe, was later to recall as the 'greatest', most memorable, of his career. Again Wales lost 3-1, mainly due to late Pelé goals in the 81st and 83rd minutes, but their performance was 'spirited', with John Charles and Hennessey once more defending well. Allchurch and substitute Ken Leek were 'always dangerous'. At one point Ivor hesitated and lost a scoring chance, but later his pass sent Woosnam away on the left; he crossed perfectly for Leek to head in a 'brilliant equaliser'. The tour ended in Mexico City where 65,000 saw their team baffle the Welsh. Antonio Jasso scored twice before being sent off together with Cliff Jones. John Charles scored a consolation goal after good work by Leek and Allchurch.

In the 1962-63 season Wales lost to Scotland at Cardiff and to England at Wembley but took some measure of satisfaction from two games against their old adversaries Hungary. It was astonishing in that period how Wales kept coming up against the same old rivals. Returning to Budapest in November 1962 Wales lost 3-1 after 'battling hard'. Once more there was considerable anxiety in anticipation of what the Magyars, hailed as one of the cleverest teams in Europe, would achieve in the second leg. Welsh confidence was already low after the 4-0 defeat at Wembley, a game of which it was said that the 'two stars Jimmy Greaves and Ivor Allchurch had stood head and shoulders above the rest'. There were now 30,000 at Ninian Park to see 'a pulsating game' in which Wales held the Hungarians to a 1-1 draw, both goals coming from penalty kicks. On the whole the visitors had dis-

*Wales v. Scotland, 1962.*
Back row: *Mal Lucas, Mel Hopkins, Tony Millington, Terry Hennessey, Mel Charles,*
*Stuart Williams. Front row: Barry Jones, Ivor, John Charles, Roy Vernon, Cliff Jones.*

appointed, but Wales, in the first half at least, were 'magnificent' and for a while, according to Bill Paton, played 'the finest and most gripping football seen in Cardiff for some time'. As in 1958 the Hungarians relied on a degree of body-checking but they also had a fine 'keeper in Szentmihalyi who provided one of the match's highlights when he brilliantly saved a drive from Ivor which had taken a deflection. In a memorable judgement Swansea's Bill Paton spoke of Ivor's 'five-star display of poise, precision and power'. He was 'without question the game's star', a verdict with which the visitors were said to concur.

Ivor was often to speak of how much he enjoyed playing against the Scots; he thought of them as 'a race which lives for football'; it was 'in their nature to *play* the game rather than to construct rigid tactics'. Looking back he was particularly to relish memories of the win at Hampden in 1951 and that at Ninian Park in October 1964. The Cardiff win, the last against Scotland for fifteen years, was a game in which Ivor 'starred', but it was chiefly remembered for two late goals by Ken Leek which ended a second half in which the Scots had been so totally in control that they made the fatal error of casually and somewhat arrogantly passing the ball to each other. Leek's first came when some of us were already behind the Canton stand on the way home; we rushed back in by the corner flag in time to see his second. It was the quickest and most timely one-two in Welsh soccer history. The mood was spoilt by a 2-1 defeat at Wembley, a poor game offering compensation only 'in the glimpses of Allchurch's undoubted class'.

Now there were more important matters in the form of qualifying matches for the 1966 World Cup which would be held in England. Wales were drawn in Group 7 along with Russia, Greece and Denmark. In the event Wales failed to qualify because they could only win their home games. Their fate was effectively sealed by a 'pathetic' 1-0 defeat in Copenhagen against the weakest team in the group. The new Welsh manager, Dave Bowen, was to regret deeply the absence from his team of both Allchurch and Roy Vernon, for this was adjudged to be 'one of the worst displays in the recent history of Welsh football'. Ivor had been suffering from a slight thigh strain and the selectors had left him at home after he had failed a fitness test on which they had insisted. Most Welsh reporters were of the view that it would have been better to have taken Ivor to Copenhagen for a late test, and that in any case he would 'have played better on one leg' than the five forwards who failed abysmally in the match. There had been no midfield retention; the defence had been given no relief.

Wales, again without Ivor, were also to lose in Athens, and so by the time Greece came to Ninian Park in March 1965 they were a team desperate for qualifying points. Only just over 11,000 fans turned up to see Wales, with Allchurch back in the Number 10 shirt, go a goal behind after only five minutes. There then followed a 'magnificent fight back' in which Ivor 'scintillated', thereby earning some of the most fulsome tributes ever paid to a Welsh international, let alone a thirty-five year old who had recently been dropped not only by his country but also by his second division club. Wales won 4-1 and were therefore 'still in the World Cup with a vengeance'. It was all due to what Dewi Lewis described as Ivor's 'astonishing performance'; Bryan Stiles thought it 'one of the most brilliant exhibitions produced by a Welsh inside forward'. Throughout, his ball control was 'incredible' and he scored a goal in each half. He had scored the equaliser when the Greek centre-half hesitated: Ivor was 'past him in a flash' and he measured his shot carefully as the goalie came out. His second came from a sudden right-footed shot after he had carefully controlled the ball and 'hoodwinked' two defenders. A goal by Roy Vernon came after Ivor had swivelled before crossing the ball from the wing. The small but enthusiastic crowd, fully aware of how privileged they were, chanted 'Ivor, Ivor'.

The Welsh team of those years, perhaps like all Welsh teams was essentially unpredictable, often seeming to lose on the swings what it had gained on the roundabouts. What does seem clear is that the team, and especially its star players, could occasionally produce that extra something when they were faced by a real challenge. This would seem the best explanation of what happened in 1965 and 1966. Following the victory against Greece, Wales retained the momentum and beat Northern Ireland 5-0 in Belfast with Ivor scoring the last goal. Then came a 4-1 defeat against Italy in Florence and a further 2-1 loss in Moscow, their last away fixture in the World Cup Group. Their next two matches were to be against England and Russia at Ninian Park. The cynics were predicting disaster, for Alf Ramsey's England seemed to be shaping up nicely for their World Cup challenge, whilst the Russians had already qualified for the finals impressively by winning all five of their previous matches in the tournament. Wales rose to the challenge and summoned up two magnificent performances, thanks very largely to the inspiration of the thirty-five year old Allchurch who travelled to both games from his new club, third-division Swansea Town. Without doubt Ivor's displays against England on 2 October 1965 and Russia on 27 October 1965 constitute a remarkable and unforgettable coda in his international career.

The England game was once again a draw, this time a goal-less one. That fact alone was an embarrassment for an England team hoping to win the 1966 World Cup for which, as hosts, they did not have to qualify. For Maurice Smith of *The People* this was 'an afternoon of shame' for first Wales had 'humiliated' England and 'then nearly thrashed them'. Few doubted that Wales had deserved to win. 'This is where we came in', groaned Smith, 'the same fumbling, shuffling, clueless England – no nearer top world-class standards than fifteen years ago when they had first entered the World Cup'. For the first time in thirty-seven years England had failed to score against Wales, a team, incidentally, fielding only five Division One players. But the overall embarrassment of the performance and the result was as nothing compared to the fact that 'the star of the game' was a thirty-five year old man with thinning blond hair who had recently joined a Third Division team for £8,000. This was the day in which England, according to their greatest ever player, Tom Finney, 'had no one in front to compare with Ivor Allchurch'; this was the day that Ivor, in the words of one historian, 'outshone the likes of Greaves, Bobby Charlton and Nobby Stiles'. Stiles had every reason to feel aggrieved, for it had been his job to mark Ivor, a task he stuck to resolutely but inadequately. Watching from the stand, Cliff Jones saw Ivor's control and body swerve bamboozle Nobby: 'he didn't know what day it was, he was completely dizzy; they say that they had to lead him off at half-time because he was so dizzy'. One of the best press photos taken that day shows Ivor shaking off Stiles and sending in a powerful shot which forced goalkeeper Springett to concede a corner. Another player outshone that day was Bobby Moore, the England captain, who was playing alongside Stiles in the half-back line. Moore later recalled Ivor's 'scintillating display' and commented not only on his 'brilliant ball control' but also on his 'generalship' of the Welsh attack. It was a day of considerable satisfaction in Wales. It had been a good team effort. Hennessey, England and Hole constituted an excellent midfield, the centre forward Wyn Davies had been a constant threat, as Bobby Moore was to attest, and on the wing Gilbert Reece, playing in place of Cliff Jones, was inspired by Ivor into making a 'dream début'. But in a thrilling game it was always Ivor himself who was catching the eye. That evening the reporters who were present were forced into composing their finest prose as they sought to do justice to what they had seen. Their efforts were totally commendable and the Allchurch fan club must have taken more satisfaction from that weekend's press than anything else in his long career. England had been made to look ordinary, said Maurice Smith, 'by the old fox Ivor'. Tudor James had thought the Welsh Number 10 had 'buzzed around like a bee at a picnic' whilst Lloyd Lewis suggested that he had 'paced the game as if fighting a fifteen round heavyweight contest; he turned and twisted with the ball and dazzled the England defence'. Nobody was more pleased that day than Swansea's Bill Paton who told his readers that Ivor had 'paced his game so perfectly' as he performed with 'the grace of a ballet dancer'. Perceptively, The *Evening Post* man pointed out that 'only a superb physical and mental approach could enable him to achieve such a performance'.

As for Ivor himself, he went out of his way to stress how good the Welsh half-back line had been: the key to the game had been the 'controlled midfield'. He confessed that he was puzzled by the current form of his club but added that playing with the Swans had been good preparation for this big match; in the Third Division the tempo was quicker and so 'I trained harder'. Meanwhile, as Ivor returned to the Vetch, Cliff Jones had gone back to Tottenham where he found his club manager Bill Nicholson unusually fulsome in his comments. Ivor's first-half performance had been 'the best inside-forward display' Nicholson 'had ever seen' and if the Swansea player 'had been younger', he told Cliff, then he would have 'broken the bank to have signed him'. Ivor's performance in what had been his fourteenth and last game against England had reverberated throughout the land. 'If Greaves is great,' concluded Lloyd Lewis, 'Allchurch is the greatest.' The last word should go to the England manager: 'Ivor,' said Alf Ramsey, 'was great out there today.'

Ivor had excelled against England but far from resting on his laurels he provided an encore. Later that month Russia came to Ninian Park, and Roger Malone of *The Daily Telegraph* was not alone in 'fearing for Wales'. Recent defeats for England and Scotland against Austria and Poland respectively had raised considerable doubts about the international standing of British football. But in front of 34,000, 'Wonderful Wales' were, in the words of Tom Lyons, 'to restore Britain's battered soccer prestige'. The previously unbeaten Russians were to lose this World Cup game 2-1, having at one stage been in the lead. It was not a classic game but the Welsh fightback generated real excitement. Jim Hill reported on how Wales 'tore into the mighty Soviet soccer masters as if this was the World Cup Final itself'. Again the midfield was the vital area and there Hole, Vernon and Allchurch had been the game's greatest creators. Bill Paton suggested that 'this team must rank as one of the best from the Principality in the post-war ear'. Chances were wasted but, said Roger Malone, Wales 'deserved a bigger victory'. This, said Jim Hill, was 'Wales' greatest soccer win'.

Roy Vernon had equalised for Wales. Meanwhile Ivor was 'striding majestically through the game' providing 'an immaculate service to his wings'. His 'brilliant' winning goal, a true 'masterpiece', came in the 77th minute after 'a lightning attack' on the left by Gilbert Reece. The winger pushed the ball into the goalmouth where, in the words of Bill Paton, Allchurch, 'seemingly hemmed in, foxed the Russian defence by swivelling round quickly and almost breaking the roof of the net with a terrific right foot drive'. Manager Dave Bowen always cited this as the best goal he had ever seen. On scoring and again at the end of the match, Ivor was mobbed by his team-mates and by the crowd. Only with great difficulty did he succeed in escaping to the dressing room from a Ninian Park pitch where he would never again be seen in the red shirt of Wales. Meanwhile Welsh football followers were left regretting their team's failure to qualify for the World Cup finals. The feeling was that Wales justly deserved to be there, perhaps more so than England. Some supporters went so far as to suggest that if Wales had qualified then perhaps a thirty-six year old Ivor Allchurch would once again be the star of the show.

In fact the great excitement of October 1965 gave way to something of an anticlimax. In November Wales lost 4-1 at Hampden in what was Ivor's last Home International. It was in this game that he also scored his last international goal, and very appropriately it was a memorable one. He raced onto a ball from Vernon, leaving the Scottish defence for dead 'before blasting the ball home via an upright'. Wales in general were flat-footed and disappointing; everyone agreed that Allchurch had been 'the best of a poor side'. A week later Ivor played his last international in Wales. On a freezing night fewer than 5,000 turned up at The Racecourse, Wrexham, to see a meaningless and irrelevant World Cup game against Denmark. The Danes were plucky but Wales won 4-2. Up front, Wyn Davies had 'stood out like a Snowdonian peak' and behind him Vernon and Allchurch 'were all verve and vitality'. Vernon scored twice and there was a goal each from Davies and winger Ronnie Rees. The Rees goal was made by Allchurch who showed 'superb control' before crossing the ball. Contrary as always, Wales, without Allchurch began 1966 by losing 4-1 to Northern Ireland at Cardiff.

The thirty-six year old Ivor Allchurch was to appear in only three more games for Wales and, perhaps not inappropriately, they were to be played in South America, the continent that by the 1960s was totally associated with the football skills of which he was a master. It seems fitting that Ivor Allchurch from Swansea should have made such an impression on Latin Americans, not least in the five games he played against Brazil. In May 1966 Brazil and Chile welcomed British opponents as they prepared for the World Cup to be held two months later in England. Playing once more in Rio, Wales lost 3-1 to a Brazil without Pelé but with Garrincha at his 'dazzling best'. Later Ivor was to describe this Brazilian team as one 'with some outstanding players' but 'failing to convince' because they 'had sacrificed some of their flair for a more physical style'. Manager Dave Bowen praised his team's efforts: Wales had started brightly largely thanks to Allchurch. Four days later Wales faced a Brazil A side in the city of Belo Horizonte and did considerably better with a fighting display. Wales lost to a single goal, a deflected free kick in the 62nd minute: shades of 1958! The Brazilian star was Jairzinho who was hailed as 'the new Garrincha' and, for Wales, goalkeeper Tony Millington was 'outstanding', as was Allchurch. Reporters spoke of the inside-forward's 'individual brilliance' and of how, in effect, he had 'led a fine Wales fight-back'. That Wales had stayed in the game for the whole ninety minutes and had even been pressing hard for a late equaliser was due to 'Allchurch's untiring efforts'.

His last game for Wales was played in the stunningly picturesque setting of Santiago, a city whose economy in the nineteenth century had largely been controlled from Swansea. Over 45,000 came to the huge stadium at the foot of the Andes to see Chile beat Wales by a single goal scored just before half-time. As the home forwards squandered chances and Wales, with Rees especially prominent, fought back, the impatient crowd booed and jeered. Their anxieties were well placed, for Chile made little impact in that summer's World Cup. Meanwhile Ivor Allchurch had flown home and a few days later he was at the Vetch to see Swansea draw their last game of the season against Brighton. A leg injury picked up in Chile prevented him from playing in that game but together with about 6,000 supporters he enjoyed watching the début of young David Gwyther who not long before had been turning out for South Gower. Swansea had its own realities. Everyone certainly agreed with Bill Paton's view that the season was too long.

Ivor had more league football to play in future seasons but he would never again play for his country. For Wales the switchback of international football was to continue with the usual mix of adventure, glory, disaster and farce. The whole venture was made worthwhile largely through the greatness of individual players. For those of us who have followed Welsh fortunes throughout the second half of the century it remains the case that any Welsh team that does not have Ivor Allchurch at inside-left looks incomplete. When he had run out wearing that red Number 10 shirt it had been the one unfailing guarantee that Wales were fit to play at international level.

# CHAPTER TEN

# *Swansong*

In May 1965, Ivor and his family moved into a new bungalow at Bishopston on the Gower peninsula. He and Esme had planned for many years to return to their roots, and once the news of the family's homecoming became common knowledge there was much speculation that Ivor was returning to the Vetch. To Ivor, and to the man-in-the-street, it made a great deal of sense that he should do so; though Cardiff City still held the Allchurch registration.

At the time, a new manager was in post at the Vetch Field. Following the relegation of Swansea Town to Division Three, Trevor Morris had been dismissed and Glyn Davies appointed in his place. Davies who had cut his managerial teeth at Yeovil Town, was a former Swansea Schoolboy, who had had a successful career at Derby County where he had captained the club. Later he had played his final seasons at the Vetch. He knew Ivor well, and had been a long-time admirer of the 'Golden Boy'. Consequently, when he heard that Cardiff were prepared to sell Ivor, Glyn Davies set out to 'get his man'.

After three weeks of negotiations, the Swansea manger agreed to pay Cardiff £8,000 for the player. There were those who believed that this was far too much to pay for a man approaching his thirty-sixth birthday, but Davies had no doubts on that score. Ivor, he believed, could play a significant role in reviving the fortunes of the Vetch field club. Apart from anything else, the name 'Allchurch, I.' Was still being included in the Welsh international team lists, and Ivor remained the same skilful, dedicated player with extensive experience and a wonderful attitude. Then, of course, there was the player's relationship with the Swansea fans. Ivor was still the idol of the Vetch Field faithful as well as of the thousands of supporters who had drifted away from the ground following his departure to Newcastle. Consequently, Glyn Davies and his directors were confident that the money which they paid to Cardiff City would be well spent. The next three seasons were to prove how right their judgement was.

*Glyn Davies gets his man.*

When Glyn Davies interviewed Ivor prior to his signing, the manager laid great emphasis upon the experience of the Vetch Field staff of the day. Notwithstanding the fact that the club had been relegated at the end of the previous campaign, eight of the Swansea team which had reached the semi-final of the F.A. Cup in 1964 were still on the club's books, and they had been joined by Irish international Willie Humphries and experienced Scot, John McGuigan. Davies argued that Ivor would bring out the best in this squad, and that the team could look forward to a successful season. The goal was promotion back to Division Two, though the manager made it clear that there was a great deal of work to be done to ensure that that objective was achieved.

On signing, Ivor said that he was delighted to be back at '. . . the club which gave me my first big chance, and I shall do my best to put back all I can into it'. And once the news of his re-signing was made public, Swansea supporters showed their delight and enthusiasm by buying season tickets in numbers which belied the club's modest station in Division Three. Indeed, by the end of July, season sales had already surpassed those purchased during the whole of the previous campaign. Hope, coupled with the warmth of their feelings for their returning hero were potent motivators for those willing buyers. Ivor, they were sure, would help the Swans back to where they rightfully belonged.

At the end of July, manager Davies announced a further signing. Former Irish international, Tommy Casey was appointed as trainer/ coach for the first team. Casey, who had played for Newcastle, Portsmouth and Bristol City, was an advocate, he said of 'traditional football'. He and Glyn Davies both believed that the then-popular 4-4-2 approach to the game had resulted in matches which were unattractive to supporters. They wanted to play a 'more open style'. Casey also said, 'I am anxious to introduce my own ideas, and try a modern approach to the game.' Later, according to Bill Paton in the *South Wales Evening Post*, Casey announced that: 'The team will revert to the swivel defence method, which will mean every player contributing to both defensive and attacking plans.' To the fans at Swansea, this sounded exciting. 'Revert', they might have thought, meant a return to the flowing football of Joe Sykes's Academy, and 5-4 games with Fulham and the like. For those fans, the season couldn't come quickly enough!

### 1965-6

Unfortunately, when the campaign began, early results were far from satisfactory. After three matches only one point had been gathered and when Shrewsbury beat the Vetch men 5-0 at Gay Meadow, it appeared as if the dismal form of the previous season was being re-enacted. Bill Paton blamed the new approach. He wrote 'The players have experienced utmost difficulty in adapting themselves to the new system and to the lower grade.' Even Ivor appeared to be adversely affected in some matches, though press reports throughout the period continued to emphasise his contribution to the team's effort. Typical of them were:

'The Swansea men could make little headway, despite the great work of Ivor Allchurch'; and 'Allchurch waged a lone battle, and

*Welsh Cup Winners, 1965-6.*
*Back row: Ken Pound, Ivor, Herbie Williams, Geo Heyes, Brian Purcell, Mike Johnson, Dai Ward.*
*Front row: Tommy Casey, Willie Humphreys, Keith Todd, Miss Paton (Mascot), Brian Hughes,*
*Glyn Davies (Manager), Jimmy McLaughlin, Roy Evans.*

despite the constant attention of several defenders, distributed the ball with the precision of old.'

Even though the team was not playing well, throughout this difficult spell there was ample evidence of the warmth of feeling which Ivor generated amongst his fans. Before the start of the first home game in which he appeared following his return, there was a special demonstration from supporters. Every one of the younger followers held up 'Welcome home Ivor' placards, whilst the older ones, no doubt wishing that they might join in that process, roared a welcome which culminated in warm applause. Later, Ivor confessed that he had more than a lump in his throat at the time.

Then came the first victory of the season – Grimsby being beaten by the only goal of the game, scored appropriately by Ivor himself. According to the *Sunday Express*, '(he) had the crowd on their toes when he beat man after man to leave Humphries clear'. The *Daily Mirror*, describing the goal, reported that: 'Allchurch scored with a deft flick of the head to get the ball between a cluster of defenders.' Jim Hill in the *Daily Express*, emphasised the effort which Ivor put into the game: 'Swansea Town fans . . . now call their idol, "Ivor the engine". The new tag sums up the ninety minutes of sweat and toil by Allchurch, as he swept Swansea to a joyful first win of the season . . . It was a non-stop, all-action Allchurch, chasing, harrying, prompting, inspiring in attack and defence.'

Sadly, the victory proved to be a false dawn, for, by the beginning of October, having been beaten 7-0 at Workington, the club was firmly entrenched at the foot of the table. At that stage of the season, seven matches had been lost of the ten played, thirty goals conceded, and only eight scored. Manager Davies was bemused. He could not understand, he said, why so many players were not achieving the levels of performance of which they were capable.

Subsequently, despite fine wins against Hull, Q.P.R. and Oldham, the Swansea men seemed unable to recover from their poor start and were struggling to extricate themselves from the basement of the league table. Ivor, however, was still attracting the attention of other managers. In December, Dave Bowen, the manager of Northampton Town and Wales, offered the Vetch club £11,000 for Ivor's services. At that time, Northampton were in the First Division, and Bowen said that he was confident that Ivor could still 'do a great job' in the highest division. 'Class will always tell!'

Given the state of affairs at the Vetch, the manager, the club and every Swans fan were delighted when Ivor told the press: 'It's very flattering to know that a first-division club wants me at my age, but I'm happy to back with Swansea.'

And the relief of the fans at that news was overlaid with great joy ten days later, when it was announced that Ivor was included in the New Year's Honours List. H.M. The Queen had awarded him an M.B.E. for services to sport. Football fans throughout the U.K. joined with their Swansea counterparts in applauding the award. For example, when Ivor ran out onto the Hull City pitch for the New Year's Day match with the home team, there was a 'spontaneous demonstration of their appreciation (from the largely home crowd) of the award for a great player'. Appropriately, it was the largest crowd to watch a match in which Ivor played that season. During the game, despite the fact that the home side (the eventual champions of the Division Three) 'were frustrated by a sturdy Swansea defensive display until the last ten minutes', every piece of Allchurch magic was applauded.

After the match, Ivor, clearly touched by the reception which he had received, responded to questions from the press about his M.B.E. by saying: 'I'm especially proud because I think that it is a tribute to football, particularly Welsh football, and to the club which started me off on my career.'

The tributes regarding the M.B.E. in the media were fulsome, though Ivor appreciated the homespun views of Bill Paton in the *South Wales Evening Post* as much as any. Paton, who had been a junior reporter when Ivor began his Vetch Field career, after congratulating him on the award, focused upon the contribution which he was making to the Swansea cause. Paton wrote:

'The £8,000 paid for Ivor Allchurch has been money well-spent. He has brought great credit to himself, to the club, and to the game by his skill and general attitude . . . He is pacing his game so that people who have a long . . . experience in and of the game, marvel at the tremendous verve and skill he puts into his play.'

And such tributes continued to flow from the pens of football commentators throughout the remainder of the season. Not surprisingly perhaps, this occurred less frequently than when he was in his prime,

*Well under control.*

but that was to be expected. In April, for example, after he had missed four matches because of calf strain, in a game against Reading, he was said to be 'back to his brilliant best, exciting the fans with his outstanding football skills' and, 'He thrilled the crowd with a corkscrew run through the Reading defence, only to be brought down in the penalty area by a desperate tackle.'

The team as a whole, though, never recovered from its poor start in the League competition. Consequently, it was the Welsh Cup which provided Ivor and his team-mates with their sole success of the season. After a two-leg final, the Swans beat Chester City at Shrewsbury to take the trophy. Again, the match reports praised Ivor's efforts. Typical of them was 'Allchurch was outstanding. Although sandwiched between two defenders he managed to blast home the winning goal.' The prize for the Swansea club was not only the Welsh Cup, but entry to Europe in the Cup Winners' Cup.

Before that though, Ivor was going to South America with the Welsh team. Amazingly, although well into his thirty-sixth year, and after an arduous season of League and Cup football, he was going to test his skills against the best of Brazil and Peru. At the *Western Mail* summed it up admirably, 'It is a tribute to his ability and dedication'.

## 1966-7

Given that Swansea Town had been unbeaten during the final six matches of the previous campaign, and had won the Welsh Cup, the 1966-7 season opened against a backcloth of cautious optimism. The positive thinkers amongst the Swansea supporters were of the opinion that, now that the Swans had got used to Division Three football, they would do well. There were new faces, too, to strengthen the squad; Vic Gomersall coming from Manchester City and Dennis Coughlin joining from Bournemouth. With the scheduled European matches adding piquancy to the prospective menu, Manager Davies, the players and the Swansea fans could have been forgiven for looking forward to a successful new campaign.

Ivor started the season playing at inside-right in order that Jimmy McLaughlin might wear the number ten shirt, and when the team drew its first match at Bristol Rovers and won the third by 3-0, things appeared to be going to plan. Unfortunately, that was not to be borne out by subsequent events. After losing the next match 1-4, only three points were gleaned from the next ten games. In every respect the situation was worrying for the Vetch management. For example, after attracting 9,752 people to the opening match, they saw 'gates' plummet to 5,000 when the Swans entertained Reading at the Vetch at the end of October. Only the novelty of the European Cup Winners' Cup tie with the Bulgarian side, Slavia, when over 12,000 people attended, brightened the financial gloom.

During this period, Ivor was nursing a groin injury and was reported as being 'off colour' during a number of games. Indeed, the *Sunday Express* account of one match reported that 'Allchurch made no impact on the game'. But, in commenting on the one which followed – a Football League Cup match at Ashton Gate – the same paper was moved to observe: 'And there was always Allchurch, belying his 37 years with another of those masterly displays of soccer craft and shooting.

Truth to tell, however, playing two games a week at thirty-seven years of age was taking its toll on Ivor. Injuries were taking longer to heal, and, given that he was playing in a side which was lacking in confidence, and was forced to play an all-action role, the physical pressures were considerable. The month of October was typical of the club's schedule at the time. The team played six League matches, a Football League Cup tie in London, and the second leg of the European tie against Slavia in Bulgaria. With all but two of these games being played away from home, the club's travel schedule added to the pressures.

During that month, however, Ivor gave the disheartened Swansea fans something to cheer about when he scored a brace of goals against Watford at the Vetch. The *South Wales Evening Post*'s description of them gives some indication of Ivor's timeless skills and his dedication to his task. The paper reported:

'Allchurch . . . left Slater helpless with a splendid shot. It was a fitting reward for real persistency', and 'Collecting the ball from the left, he swivelled around and let loose a drive which left the goalkeeper gasping as it scorched into the corner of the net.'

Unfortunately, by that time, Swansea Town was propping up the rest of the teams in the Division Three table. With a third of the season having elapsed, the club had scraped together just six points.

*Esme, John and David with Ivor, M.B.E.*

There was, too, dissatisfaction at board level with the lack of effort by certain team members during the second leg of the Cup Winners' Cup match in Bulgaria. According to two of the directors, who had accompanied the team, some players did not try. Subsequently, the board announced that 'We have had a searching enquiry and have taken action which will be in the best interests of everyone.' The wording was ominous.

Days later, the club announced that Glyn Davies and Tommy Casey had had their contracts terminated by 'mutual consent'. Davies wished the club every success in the future and handed over the reins to the sixty-eight year-old Joe Sykes, who was appointed as Caretaker Manager. Walter Robins was to be his trainer and Ivor was to be part of the selection committee. As so often happens in such circumstances, after five weeks without a win, in the next match the side defeated Reading by 5-2. In this game, according to the press, 'Ivor came in for some rough treatment from Reading defenders, but probed and prompted in a majestic way.'

Sadly, thereafter, the Swans defence continued to leak goals at an alarming rate. Indeed, after the club had played 29 matches, the 'goals against' column totalled 64. Such was the crisis that, just before the Boxing Day match against Shrewsbury, Joe Sykes asked Ivor to take on the captaincy. According to Joe, Brian Prucell, the club centre-half, who had been captain, was not playing to the best of his ability because of the weight of the responsibility of captaincy. Ivor replied that he was glad to help not only his old mentor, but also Brian and the club. He told the press, 'This season, the team has lost confidence, and when Mr Sykes asked me, I thought that it would be better if I, as the most experienced player, took over.'

The change appeared to have had the desired result, for the first three games under the new captain provided the club with two wins and a draw. The most notable of the victories was that over Oxford Utd. on their own ground, the Swans' first away victory of the campaign. The Swans were losing 0-2 at half time, but after what one of the players called 'A half-time tongue lashing from Ivor of which few thought him capable', in the second period the side was transformed. In that half, the Swans scored three goals without reply, and the skipper had a foot in each of them. He was, reported the *Daily Express*, 'the outstanding forward on the field. He was supreme!' And, years later, according to a certain 'R. Atkinson', who marked him that day, 'He was incredible for his age. What skill! What stamina!'

The victory took the Swans off the bottom of the table, and was one reason why there was a little more confidence at the Vetch Field at that time. Apart from anything else, the Oxford match was the sixth in succession without a defeat. Nevertheless, too many goals were still being conceded, and, following a defeat at Scunthorpe and a further run of three matches without losing, seven games produced just two points.

By then, however, Joe Sykes had been relieved of his command as a result of the appointment of Billy Lucas as the Swans manager. Lucas had been in the Swansea side when Ivor made his League début, he had played with him for Wales, and knew the Swansea star better than most. On his arrival, Lucas had said that he would have to 'lean heavily on Joe Sykes and Ivor Allchurch for the first few weeks. They have a wealth of soccer know-how.' In spite of their knowledge, and no matter how hard they worked with the squad available to them, the Lucas-Sykes-Allchurch triumvirate could not steer the Swansea ship to safety. Even though they won five of their last ten matches, at the end of the season Swansea Town could not avoid relegation to Division Four.

Such was the gloom in Swansea, that only 4,687 bothered to turn up for the last match of the campaign, which, as it happened, was a fine 4-1 win over Walsall. Those who were there, however, witnessed an historic happening; Ivor appeared with number six on his back. Manager Lucas had himself been converted to a half-back in the twilight of his career, and asked Ivor if he would try the same thing as an experiment. It was one which was not to be repeated; by the time the next season started, Lucas had decided to use Ivor in a different role.

Disappointing as the season's outcome was, it is clear from the playing statistics that Ivor Allchurch made a handsome contribution to the Swansea cause during the campaign. He appeared in 54 League and Cup matches, and, despite working hard in mid-field and in defence, scored more goals than any other Swansea player. As Billy Lucas put it at the time, 'He never spared himself. He gave all he had for the team.'

Later, a journalist suggested to Ivor that, had the side gathered a similar proportion of points from its first fourteen games as were gained from the remainder, the club would not have been relegated. It was an intriguing idea, but it could not alter the harsh fact of relegation. Division Four football loomed. Hardly, as the fates were to decree, a fitting stage for one of the world's greatest footballers to play out his final season.

### 1967-8

When the 1967-8 campaign began, Ivor was approaching his 38th birthday. Consequently, it was a credit to his fitness and dedication as well as his skills that he was able to offer so much on the altar of Swansea football during the season which lay ahead. In all, he played thirty-eight League matches and seven cup ties during the campaign and scored twenty-one goals in the process (including his final League 'hat-trick'). He was also a member of the Swans team which, in doing battle in the F.A. Cup with first-division Arsenal, attracted a record 'gate' of 32,786 to the Vetch. It is true that he made this contribution in the lowest division in the Football League, but the effort was nonetheless remarkable. And, as many were to observe as the season wore on, he played with dignity and grace, as well as great skill throughout what was a long and arduous campaign.

Before the season started, Ivor was approached regarding the possibility of extending his contract by a further year. At the time he was undecided and, before making up his mind, resolved to see how he stood up to another long season of competitive football. He still loved playing the game, almost as much as he had done when he first came to the Vetch, but *anno domini* was beginning to take its toll. In addition, he was beginning to wonder whether he should continue, having in mind the idea which was troubling him that by carrying on he might be blocking the progress of younger players. He said at the time, 'I can't go on for ever, and I was given my chance as a youngster. I don't want to get in the way of a young player who needs the experience to develop.' No one at the Vetch – nor among the club's dwindling band of supporters would have agreed with Ivor on that count, though they might have understood his concern. In the event, the Vetch management was to make up Ivor's mind for him. Soon after the end of the season, he was told that a further one-year contract was on offer; however, he would have to agree to a reduction in his wages from £40.00 to £35.00. Ivor was aggrieved at that; though it was not so much the loss of the £5.00 per week which disturbed him so much as the thought of the offer being indicative of a penny-pinching attitude by the Vetch management towards a man who had rendered the club exceptional service. Whether Ivor would have retired anyway can never be known. In retrospect, though, setting aside the small-minded thinking, it does seem to have been a foolish attempt by the management to save £5.00 per week when in the process they dismayed their most senior professional and lost their leading goal-scorer and most eminent player, plus a great deal of good will.

None of this had surfaced, however, when, during July 1967, Ken Jones, the Chief Soccer Writer of the *Daily Mirror* wrote a fulsome tribute to Ivor in his paper. In it, Jones quoted the opinion of numerous football gurus regarding the Swansea favourite. He finished his article with the following paragraph:

> 'In the autumn of 1965, less than a year before England won the World Cup, Ivor lined up against Alf Ramsey's rapidly emerging

*'In it goes!' – Brian Hughes and Roy Evans are 'the gallery'.*

team. Ramsey, seldom liberal with his praise, rated him "The man of the game". Since Ivor was well into his thirty-fifth year at the time, that was praise indeed.' Jones went on to say that Ivor had graced the game for many seasons, and, although he was about to play in Division Four for the first time, a new set of audiences would be able to enjoy the skills of the Allchurch game. 'Class,' argued Jones, 'will always shine through.'

In their discussions before the start of the campaign, Billy Lucas had told Ivor that he wanted him to play 'more as a striker. Leave some of the running around to the younger legs.' And Ivor was happy to oblige, though, given his nature, there were many occasions during the season when he covered more ground than his younger colleagues. Lucas, however, recognising the need for goals to win matches, was wise enough to give his most senior player more scope to attack opposing defences. And, if we are to judge simply by the number of goals he scored, the Lucas ploy met the need admirably.

The new season started with a Vetch Field match against Bradford (Park Avenue), when a crowd of 7,418 saw the sides share the points. There followed a win over Doncaster, in which Ivor scored, and a run of four matches without defeat, including a 2-2 draw with eventual champions, Luton Town. After ten matches had been played, the side lay in mid-table, having earned ten points. Even though the team was hardly setting the world on fire, at least the defence was being more effective; only Barnsley managed to score three against them, and that in Yorkshire. With several promising youngsters coming into the side, Billy Lucas felt that he was beginning to make progress with his team-building. Gates, however, still left much to be desired. After a crowd of 7,418 attended the opening game, by the beginning of October, only 4,241 came to see the side draw 1-1 with York City.

Nonetheless, Ivor's play continued to attract favourable press comment. Of a match at Doncaster, the *Western Mail* reported that, 'Allchurch did a great deal of intelligent grafting and prompting and scored a superb goal.' Against Brentford, he was said to have: 'Coolly glided in Humphries' centre for the fifth goal', whilst, in the next match, at Southend, 'the Allchurch know-how stood out like a beacon, whether it was helping out a harassed defence or trying to get his forwards moving.'

The next three matches in which he scored are also worthy of comment, for they reveal all too clearly how dubious is a myth which has grown about Ivor. Even those who played with him for many seasons say that he would only head the ball *in extremis*. Yet, consider the following descriptions of Allchurch goals which were scored in the first half of that 1967-8 season. 'Todd's chip was delicately nodded in to the Bradford net by Allchurch'; Coughlin floated a perfect centre in the closing minutes from which Allchurch headed a superb goal'; and, 'Allchurch glanced a Screen cross beyond the diving goalkeeper.'

These descriptions are not unusual. Rather, they are typical of many goals which Ivor scored. Indeed, our analysis of the total of 251 League goals which he scored for the three clubs for whom he played, shows that almost fifteen percent were converted with his head. It is true that most of them were 'placed' with a subtlety which was in keeping with the elegance of his football. Some, however, were headed home with a power of which a Ford or Lawton would have been proud.

One such goal was witnessed by the Swansea City manager, John Hollins, when, as a youth he had gone to see his brother play for Newcastle against the 'Spurs 'Double' side. John's abiding memory of that game was that he was left in awe of an Allchurch goal. It seems that Ivor was outside the Tottenham penalty area when he connected with the ball with his head so firmly that it 'flashed into the home goal like a rocket!'

Goals also came thick and fast for the maestro in the December of 1967. Partly as a result of manager Lucas's wisdom in 'resting' Ivor for two November matches when he had a slight thigh strain, and using him only as a substitute for the next two matches, when December came Ivor was fresh. On December 16, at Bradford (P.A.), he scored 'two great goals'; and 'stamped his quality and authority on the proceedings'. The following week, he went one better, scoring his final League hat-trick against Doncaster, which the *Daily Mail* referred to as 'Vintage Allchurch'. And, three days later he was one of the scorers against Newport County, thus scoring six goals in three successive games, which at thirty-eight was some record.

Ivor also took his purple patch of form into the F.A. Cup competition. He scored a goal in the defeat of Brighton, and was involved in both goals by which Doncaster were defeated in the next round. That victory put the Swans 'in the hat' with the major sides, and the fates decreed that they were to play Arsenal at the Vetch. The old enthusiasm returned to Swansea and people who had not seen the club play for many seasons returned in droves. The majority remembered the 1950 match in London when the Swans had given the 'Gunners' the 'fright of their lives'. That, of course, was the match which brought Ivor Allchurch to the attention of football's world at large, when the Arsenal manager had called him 'The player of the century'. As it happened, that was Ivor's first game in the competition. Now, at thirty-eight, he was to do battle with the London giants once again. Had those Swansea fans known that it was to be their hero's final F.A. Cup game, the romantics among them would have read much into the matter. Stars and tea leaves would, no doubt, have been consulted and unfavourable omens ignored.

The Arsenal side, then standing in the upper regions of the First Division, were strong favourites to win the game. Their defence, it was said, was amongst the best in the game, with players like McLintock, Neil and Ure prominent. As the match progressed, Ivor found that he had a constant companion in Ure, who, when necessary called on Neil and a retreating Graham. Nonetheless, Ivor made his presence felt, though it was the 'New Ivor', Herbie Williams, who, every Swansea supporter would argue to this day, prised open the Gunners' defence to release Keith Todd who 'scored'. The referee thought otherwise and when Bobby Gould headed home a fine goal, the Swans were out of the F.A. Cup competition. This time, Whittaker and Alex James and hyperbole were absent, but every Arsenal defender shook Ivor's hand warmly at the final whistle, whilst Bertie Mee was 'more than polite with his praise for the veteran Swansea man.'

That match helped to fill the depleted Swansea coffers, but, in effect, it ended the club's season. Despite a run of five matches without defeat in December, thereafter results left much to be desired and, whilst safely placed in mid-table, at the end there was nothing but pride to play for. As ever, Ivor gave his all in that cause. Against Lincoln in March, it was reported that 'Allchurch ran himself to a standstill in a vain effort to bring about some co-ordination, and scored an outstanding goal'. Ivor headed two goals against Southend, and against Chesterfield he and Herbie Williams were said to have 'worked tremendously hard to break down the home defence'. He scored in that match, too, and the *Daily Mirror* recorded that 'Allchurch's goal was a magnificent effort, hit on the volley, rising into the roof of the net.'

That goal turned out to be Ivor's last in League football. Fittingly, it was scored at the Vetch and was stamped with his characteristic 'trade-mark'; a volley struck with venom. He was to play just one more League match; that against Hartlepools United, again at the Vetch, on 6 May 1968. At that time, when pressed by people from the media about retirement, he remained non-committal. He was, he said, 'keeping his options open'. Consequently, the Swansea public were not aware that that match with Hartlepools was to be Ivor's last for the club. The 3,491 who bothered to turn up had no inkling that they were witnessing a game of special significance.

Some of those who were there had had the great privilege of marvelling at him in his prime; others had only seen him in the twilight of his career. Later, however, when Ivor announced his retirement, all who had been there on that memorable day to witness the curtain fall on the career of a truly great player – many would say, Swansea Town's greatest ever – could boast of the fact! That Fourth Division match hardly did justice to the end of so notable an epoch in the history of the club. Yet, little as the Swans had to play for that day, there were numerous magical touches and much endeavour from the tall, elegant Allchurch. This man, of whom Matt Busby said: 'He never needed a number on his back. His polish and his class could not be missed,' played his heart out to the end. His class could not be missed, but he himself would be, for his like would never be seen again.

# CHAPTER ELEVEN

# *Valediction*

When Ivor played against the 50-year-old Stanley Matthews at Ninian Park in 1962 he must have wondered which team's colours he would be wearing when his own half-century came around. He might not have guessed that it would be Pontardawe, that he would be playing in the Second Division of the Welsh League, and that, appropriately enough, the colours he would be wearing would be the black and white stripes that he had graced at Newcastle. Unlike Sir Stanley, Ivor had not kept going as a Football League player, but nevertheless his love of the game and his careful tending of his skills allowed him to go on playing good meaningful and competitive soccer for twelve years after his last League game. That having finally left the Swansea he should go on playing first with Worcester City and then in Wales with Haverfordwest as player-manager, and finally, after a short break, with Pontardawe would have surprised none of his family and friends. As Ken Jones, who had been a colleague at the Vetch before becoming a leading sporting columnist, so perceptively noted, 'People like Ivor don't retire,' because for him 'football wasn't a game it was a way of life.'

As Ivor approached his fiftieth birthday in 1979 the *Observer Magazine* sent Alan Road to see him play for Pontardawe against Ynysybwl. Road joined a crowd of '17 men and the obligatory dog' at the tree-lined recreation ground, and heard manager Dixie Hale say that he had signed Allchurch for 'his class and experience'. Both qualities were in evidence that day for Ivor 'scored two goals, plotted a third and was seen in most corners of the pitch during the course of a warm afternoon'; his team won 5-0. At this time what little hair Ivor had left was silver but his frame was lean and, wearing the familiar magpie stripes, it was too easy for the London-based reporter to believe 'that the clock had been turned back'. Earlier as he had entered the ground, Road had seen the great man arrive alone and stride in 'looking rather like the ageing Western hero summoned from out of town to solve some local difficulty with a little judicious shooting'. He explained that he still trained twice a week with his local team at Bishopston on Gower and that even if he had not signed for Pontardawe he would be out running or doing something physical. Obviously, to play was better; 'I just love it!' he confessed.

The national press were to take one last look at Ivor the player in 1980. He had finally and formally retired in that year and when Esme Allchurch made him burn his boots it did look as if he had at last come to terms with what Ken Jones had described as 'the evil day'. But to celebrate the Centenary of the Welsh Rugby Union a special match was arranged between Welsh soccer and rugby players. This unique occasion allowed the Cardiff Arms Park crowd to relish the coming together of the stars of both codes, to see Gareth Edwards and Phil Bennett in opposition to John Toshack and Mike England. Ivor played in that match and that was something which gave special pleasure to reporter Rob Hughes who took the opportunity to tell readers of the *Herald Tribune* just how magnificent the great inside-forward's gifts had been. At the Arms Park that day Ivor's head was now that of an ageing man, and that 'surge that had taken him past two or three opponents has mellowed into a gracious trot', but the torso was still lean and 'the Allchurch hallmarks' were all still in evidence, 'the refined control, passing and finishing'. For Hughes, Ivor would always be re-membered for 'his amazing grace;' and for being 'elegance personified'.

What struck reporters more than anything as they watched the 51 year-old play that day was the contrast with the greed of modern players. At the time when both domestic stars and European internationals were refusing to play unless paid huge bonuses, Allchurch was taken to exemplify an older attitude in which players simply rejoiced in their love of the game 'He would play anywhere for any amount,' said Hughes. 'Playing soccer,' Ivor told him was 'a lovely life.' Even then he was still enjoying it, 'I like to hit the ball, to stroke it along nicely.' Commenting on the modern game he very much hoped that young players would 'Go out and give 100 percent because of the enjoy-ment.' His advice was, 'You've got to love the game.'

Everyone was impressed not only by Ivor's fitness, Rob Hughes thought that 'he was in the pink', but also by the stability and whole-someness of his home life. He and Esme were living if not anony-mously then quietly and comfortably in their bungalow at Bishopston. He was working as a storeman in a stationery warehouse. He still

*Ivor and sons – training.*

trained a couple of times a week and enjoyed playing squash and tennis. The surrender to golf would come a little later. He was always, as a spectator, to follow the sporting careers of his two sons and seemed more than happy that they had put their families first by opting to play for local teams. He admitted to Rob Hughes that he was a regular supporter at the Vetch but suggested that various pressures had changed the nature of the game. 'I preferred our style,' he explained, 'we put our foot on the ball, looked around, whereas they do tear about more.' In a later interview with the *Newcastle Evening Chronicle*, he recalled Matthews, Finney and Pelé as the opponents who had impressed him most, and though there was much talk of 'declining standards' he pointed to Gary Lineker and Paul Gascoigne of Spurs as two 'excellent' contemporary players.

Ivor Allchurch professional footballer had become Ivor Allchurch storeman. Meantime, of course, he had also become a soccer legend. Journalists had continued writing about Ivor throughout the 1970's. The fulsome tributes, which had been paid to him in his 1967 Testimonial Brochure and in particular, the comments of Matt Busby and Bobby Moore were to be the basis of many subsequent assessments. In 1973 the *Sun* newspaper began a series with three great masters of the pass – Alex James, Ernie Taylor and Ivor Allchurch, but in their layout they gave prominence to the latter. A dramatic photograph of Ivor in Newcastle colours was accompanied by the headline, 'Better than Pelé by a mile'. This was the claim made by the then current Welsh manager, Dave Bowen who was the newspaper's main source for their article. Bowen who was always to be one of Ivor's greatest champions held nothing back as he enthused about 'the greatest inside-forward since the war'. Bowen had 'played against them all – Pelé, di Stefano, Liedholm – and Ivor was the best.' He recalled Ivor's great goal against Russia, his great passes across five or fifty yards, and how 'he could beat people as if they didn't exist'. For Bowen, Ivor 'was the complete inside-forward' a player with 'fantastic feet, wonderful technique, the perfect build and a marvellous composure.'

The attention to Ivor in print was accompanied by and indeed prompted debate, discussion, reminiscence and argument. Soccer legends are highlighted in the press but they are created in homes where fathers talk to sons, in pubs where mates and strangers shuffle memories and in those formal dinners where uncomfortable looking men in dinner jackets like to get their money's worth by mingling with the great. These were the milieu in which the name Allchurch was kept alive. Again and again his skills would be explained, comparisons would be made, and if Ivor himself was present, as he often was at dinners held to honour him or his football friends, he would be asked for his views about who was the greatest. What was particularly pleasing about these sporting dinners was that Ivor would take his place alongside the greats of other sports. At functions organised by the

Welsh Sports Hall of Fame to which he was inducted, or the Swansea Sportsmen's Club, he would not only enjoy the company of boxers like Jack Petersen, Howard Winstone and Colin Jones, but he would hear rugby stars like Carwyn James, Barry John and Gareth Edwards confess to a love of soccer and admit that to a considerable degree their own skills, especially ball skills, had been inspired by watching Ivor Allchurch at the Vetch. It was particularly gratifying for Ivor, who had beaten Howard Winstone to become *Welsh Sports Personality of the Year* back in 1962, to realise the extent to which in the years following his retirement he had become a legend not only for veteran supporters at the Vetch, Ninian Park or St. James's Park but also for the sporting community as a whole.

All the while, of course, in a remarkable social phenomenon football nostalgia was intensifying. In part this was related to a massive commercial exploitation of the game as newspapers, book publishers, television companies and manufacturers of related products realised that there were fortunes to be made out of the people's game. Mercifully, all this commercial hype was accompanied by the granting to football of a new intellectual respectability. Football journalists were encouraged to rise above clichés and in the wake of Nick Hornby, novelists were given considerable advances as they attempted to explain how their particular anxieties had been formed during wet afternoon on exposed terraces. Ivor Allchurch together with some of his great contemporaries were no longer being recalled merely as soccer legends. Now they were becoming significant cultural icons.

The *Weekly News* thought that the end of the 1970's was a good time to celebrate fifty years of League football by identifying '*The Fifty Greatest Players*'. The status of Welsh football at the time is reflected in the fact that five of the fifty were Welsh. Ivor was there, along with Ronnie Burgess, John Charles, Bryn Jones and Roy Paul. The alphabet ensured that Allchurch headed the whole list and of him it was said that he was 'a touch payer with a giant-sized heart'. Ivor's own particular favourites, Raich Carter and Peter Doherty, to whom he was often compared, were also on the list. Of Doherty it was said that he was 'electrifying when in full cry', but of Carter, giant that he was, it was remarked that he was 'almost as good as he thought he was'. Lists and charts of this nature are the very stuff of a nations' identity and there are many British citizens who think of Peter Jeffs' 1991 study of *The Golden Age of Football* as being as crucial to any understanding of post-war Britain as the works of professional historians such as K. O. Morgan and Peter Hennessy. Amongst the sixty or so players highlighted by Jeffs were Walley Barnes, Trevor Ford, Roy Paul, Alf Sherwood, Roy Burgess, John Charles and Ivor Allchurch. Of Ivor it is said that 'at club level he was often in a higher class than most of his colleagues', and that he was 'clearly the outstanding discovery in Welsh football in this post-ware era.'

Former players were also reluctant to let the Allchurch legend fade. In 1978, Jimmy Hill who, when playing for Fulham alongside Johnny Haynes, had encountered Ivor in many games, chose to begin his alphabetical treatment of *The Great Soccer Stars* by recalling the Swansea man's great qualities. 'He had elegance,' explained Hill, 'the game never seemed to be going too fast for him' and 'he was a lovely fluent mover, so fluent that he did not change gears, he was always in automatic drive.' Of course, the former Fulham inside-forward had to indulge in a little punditry as he pointed out that Ivor 'was not the greatest defender in the true sense of the phrase', but to his eternal credit he went on to wonder 'how many wing-halves who were supposed to be looking after him found time for attacking duties?'

A decade later, Trevor Brooking also nodded in the direction of contemporary managerial speak when he referred to Ivor's lack of defensive awareness, but naturally the former West Ham and England inside-forward was eager to point out that he himself had learnt from watching the Welshman. Of course, Brooking had noticed his 'time on the ball', his 'unhurried style', but what had been vital to his whole game was that 'his first touch was always clean'; it was that which gave Ivor time to control the ball and to pass so tellingly. The two players had much in common but Brooking, for all his magisterial presence and effective passing never had Ivor's pace or finishing ability.

Overall, the Allchurch reputation was in good hands. His name, and it always helps for a sporting legend to have a distinctive name, sometimes pronounced 'Allchurch' and other times 'Al Church', was honoured in conversation and in print. Nostalgia intensified the predilection for lists and so it came about that as the Millennium approached and the Football League wanted to commemorate 1998-9 as their Centenary year, a list of *'100 League Legends'* was identified. This time there were eight Welshmen. Some were disappointed that players like Roy Paul and Mark Hughes were excluded but there was particular satisfaction in Swansea for four of its sons had been selected. What had been such a remarkable era of schoolboy football in the west Wales town was very appropriately honoured by the inclusion in this distinguished roll call of Trevor Ford, John Charles, Cliff Jones and Ivor Allchurch.

Three of these Swansea boys were alive to enjoy the honour, but Ivor had died a year earlier on July 9 1997 aged 67. He had been just five months short of equalling the number of his international caps. Until the year before his death, Ivor had still been seen at games and at dinners, he had talked about his golf and boasted about his three beautiful granddaughters and a handsome grandson. On these occasions, as always, he had been modest, reserved, quietly elegant and circum-spect. In his sixties he had taken on something of a clerical air and in many ways his refined manner and somewhat nervous smile would have suited him had be carried out the duties of a vicar in a Gower Parish. In time, however, we heard the rumours of his illness and we knew that a body that had never let him down as a player was under attack. Whilst his friends, loved ones and earnest fans may have been prepared for his death, it still came no only as a shock but as a re-minder to a whole community that it had lost one of its greatest sons. Immediately a whole city realised that it was to have to honour a man who had lived so unassumingly and self-effacingly in one of its suburbs. Amongst the five hundred mourners at Morriston Crematorium on that day in July 1997 were many who had travelled long distances to be there, but it was overwhelmingly a Swansea day as the city paid tribute to its greatest sportsman. Clive Rowlands and Don Shepherd represented Swansea's wider sporting interests and manager Jan Molby was joined by the directors and players of Swansea City Football Club. But it was the former Swans who seemed so fittingly to sum up what the day meant. Esme, Len Allchurch and the family as a whole took considerable solace from the presence of Swans giants such as Trevor Ford, Mel Charles, Mel Nurse and Terry Medwin. The appre-ciation was given by Tom Kiley, who recalled a fifty-year friendship in football. How was it, he asked, that Ivor who had thrilled crowds of 60,000 or more would refuse to play his golf shots at Ashleigh Road until the Mumbles Train had moved on?

Swansea had honoured its own, but the football nation as a whole was not slow in paying *its* tributes. It had been interesting to note how soccer's new fashionable status had been reflected in the broadsheet obituary columns. The passing of the 'Golden Age' football greats is now marked in very much the same way as the death of a statesman or filmstar. The sight of Nat Lofthouse, Sir Stanley Matthews, Tom Finney and Jackie Mudie forming a guard of honour at the funeral of Stanley Mortenson allowed a whole culture to reflect on its elements and to confirm its pantheon. Similarly, Ivor's death allowed football followers throughout the United Kingdom to reflect on what constituted football excellence and what it was that was most appealing and memorable in the national game. He had only played 103 of his 694 League matches at the top level, said *The Times* of Ivor, 'yet', it continued, 'his gifts were incomparable'. In a short paragraph of stunning economy and exquisite accuracy *The Times* referred to Ivor's 'balance, style, elegant feet and surge of pace', as well as his 'mesmerising dribbling' and 'precision passing' which could be rounded off 'by the fiercest of shots'. In the *Independent* he was called 'an exceptional footballer' and 'a classic inside-forward' who was 'a master of the defence splitting pass' and 'whose goals resulted from the violent accuracy of his long-range shooting'.

In these national obituaries there was a veritable note of regret. In the *Independent* his former Wales colleague, Cliff Jones, was quoted as saying that he was sure 'that if he'd gone to a big English club earlier we'd be speaking about one of the all-time greats.' Ivor's career had often been interpreted in this way. In one of his many appreciations, Rob Hughes referred to how he 'had frittered away the best years of his youth trying year after year after year to guide his beloved Swansea up to the élite First Division.' As we argued earlier in this book, perhaps Ivor should have gone to, say, Manchester United in his mid-twenties. That was his favourite ground and he always treasured memories of a match there which ended 4-4 after Newcastle had been 4-1 down at half time. Of course he loved playing the sport in front of huge knowledgeable crowds and, just as they had at Newcastle, they would have loved him at the stadium where later his fellow-countrymen Mark Hughes and Ryan Giggs were to be adored. Certainly, analysing Ivor's career lends itself perfectly to the 'What if?' game. But to dwell on a note of regret is to misunderstand both that career and the age in which it was lived.

In football's 'Golden Age', as we have seen, the game was played and played skilfully throughout the length and breadth of the land. Commercial hype had not yet allowed two or three glamour clubs to

escape into the stratosphere where they could entertain thoughts of breaking with a national league structure. Of course, there were glamour clubs, we all know about the Arsenal's marble halls, but most fans thought their own local team as good as, if not better than any other you could care to name. Most fans certainly thought of themselves as the most knowledgeable and therefore the best judge of players. In an industrial, as compared to a post-industrial society there was a far more equitable geographical distribution of jobs, capital and confidence. There was every reason to believe that glory could be achieved at Burnley, Sunderland, Hull, Portsmouth or Swansea.

There was also the maximum wage regulation, which meant that there was no obvious and legal incentive for players to leave their families and friends. Indeed, given the opportunities for local journalism and friendship with local business interest it often made much more sense to be a big fish in a little pond rather than to risk playing in the company of temperamental super-stars. It was not thought at all strange that in *Charles Buchan's Football Monthly* and in the Christmas albums that Allchurch was identified with Swansea just as Sam Bartram belonged to Charlton, Wilf Mannion to Middlesborough and Jimmy Hagan to Sheffield United. It might additionally have been the case that Ivor's international career meant that there was less incentive for him to move. From 1950 on he was in the international limelight and was collecting his match fees from every game. This at a time when so many talented inside-forwards could not get into the English team. Raich Carter's career was greatly disturbed by the War, but it is stunning to realise that he only won 13 England caps. Ivor Broadis only played 14 times for his country, Len Shackleton won only five caps and Jimmy Hagan, who often played in Wartime games, won only one full cap. It was an age with very different expectations from that of the television era, an age too, in which there were very different satisfactions. For a Welshman there was also the question whether a League club based in England would be prepared to release him for international duty for his country.

Yet ultimately Ivor's career was a reflection of his own personality and clearly he was not an aggressive pusher who thought that the world owed him affluence. He gave no evidence of craving publicity, of wanting special treatment or of wishing to display conspicuous consumption. Just as he was at ease with the ball so too he had come to terms with his body and his job. His physical gifts allowed him to become an exceptional professional footballer. It was entirely natural and satisfying for him to discipline his life so that he could enjoy playing and in so doing entertain the paying customers. His was an attitude towards living and working which was entirely common in the working-class culture of which he was a product. His skills were understood to be natural qualities that allowed satisfaction within a culture and within a community rather than outside of these spheres. Fulfilment was the goal not escape or transcendence.

All his life Ivor knew that his ability to control a football had meant one thing more than any other. It meant that he did not have to work in the local I.C.I. factory with other members of his family. He was a working-man whose skills had allowed him to make a living as an entertainer. He was a shy man of few words. He liked a quiet drink and a game of darts but he would never be the life and soul of the party. If he was to appear in public he would be perfectly happy to let his feet do the talking. If he was to be a public figure it would be as a footballer. He could please himself and others by doing what he did best, just as other working-men living in the same street would win prizes with their roses or from playing snooker. He was a true professional not only because he earned a living by doing something well, but because he knew exactly the role and place in society that his fabulous skills had given him.

It was a working-class culture that demanded professionalism more than any other quality, but, at the same time, it valued and appreciated excellence. Football fans longed for excitement and usually this was associated with goalmouth action. They wanted goals at one end and saves at the other. But they also wanted something in between and *that* they took to be the essence of the game. A team would be deemed to be 'a good footballing side' if they provided lots of build-up before their goals. Fans wanted their team to be identified as 'a good footballing side' almost as much as they wanted success in cup or league. And to have such a side one needed men who were continually referred to as 'ball-artists'. In a working class culture in which some men could sing or play the piano or breed pigeons or even make a billiard ball talk, others were expected to be football wizards. The whole game of football would only work, would only satisfy if the fearless tacklers, the speedy wingers, and the sure-fire marksmen could be orchestrated by 'the real footballers', the men whose balance, control, poise and vision allowed the undoing of defences. Uniquely these artists, these wizards, were players in whom physical skill and football intelligence had combined to bestow a special grace. Such a player was Ivor John Allchurch. He rarely played a game in which he failed to give the crowd the pleasure of seeing what they took to be the best things in the sport. His control of the ball seemed to defy normal mechanics. Then he would proceed to beat, to outwit, to ghost past opponents. All the time he was scheming, trying new things, new tricks and turns to break down defences. All this was done with an elegance that the crowd had eagerly anticipated. By then they were beginning to feel that they had been given their money's worth. But then suddenly Ivor would give them a bonus. Whilst running towards the opposing box, and without breaking his stride, he would unleash a powerful right-footed or left-footed shot. Sometimes one wondered whether he just scored these spectacular goals to show the other forwards how it should be done.

There was a natural rhythm to Ivor's game and somehow when he was in our team that rhythm extended to the side as a whole. Come sun or come rain, come the top-of-the-league side or a bunch of no-hopers from a town one couldn't place geographically, Ivor would be there to entertain us and to make us feel important. When the younger of the present authors first came to Swansea and to the Vetch, he automatically assumed that the local pub called 'The Ivorites' was the headquarters of a fan club. In those days we were certainly all Ivorites. We both saw him play great games at the Vetch and Ninian Park but as we researched the material for this volume we began to wonder why we hadn't made more effort to see him at Worcester, Haverfordwest and Pontardawe. As ageing middle-aged men we know that we speak for many of our contemporaries but we sincerely hope that there are younger people too who cherish the memory of Ivor's skills.

In that respect we draw enormous comfort from Len Pitson's wonderful photograph of Ivor's last game at the Vetch – his Testimonial – for as he tries to leave the field he is clearly engulfed by hundreds of excited and adoring youngsters. You can bet that they had all been urged by their father or grandfather to go and say farewell to the great man. We both loved to watch him play and we loved too the natural dignity and modesty of the great man. This book is our way of saying thank you to Ivor for the pleasure he gave not only to us but to countless others! For showing so clearly that every game of football, at whatever level provides the opportunity for the skilful player to scheme effec-

*Ivor and young fans at his Testimonial Match, 1968.*

tively, fairly, thrillingly and beautifully. And for exemplifying all that is good about the true club man. There can never be another Ivor Allchurch, but we hope that this book will provide its older readers with a lasting memory of this footballing genius and that, for younger fans, it may help in some small way to make up for the fact that they were not privileged to see the great man play.

*'In retrospect' – Ivor receives a silver salver to mark his 68 International appearances.*

THE APPENDICES

# Ivor's Career Statistics

The following section contains four parts; one relating to each of the clubs for whom he played and one to his appearances for Wales: They are presented in alphabetic order, i.e.:

CARDIFF CITY
NEWCASTLE UNITED
SWANSEA TOWN
WALES

## At Cardiff City (1962-5)

Ivor joined the Bluebirds from Newcastle United in July 1962. He made his club début versus Newcastle on 18th August 1962. The match resulted in a 4-4 draw. The team on that occasion was: John, Harrington, Milne, Hole, Rankmore, Baker, McIntosh, Durban, Charles (M.), Allchurch, Hooper.

### IVOR'S LEAGUE AND CUP APPEARANCES
### AND GOALS FOR CARDIFF CITY

| Season | Div | League | | FA Cup | | FL Cup | | Welsh Cup | | Euro CW Cup | |
|--------|-----|--------|-----|--------|-----|--------|-----|-----------|-----|-------------|-----|
| | | App | Gls | App | Gls | App | Gls | App | Gls | App | Gls |
| 1962-3 | 2 | 35 | 12* | 1 | – | 1 | – | 2 | 2 | – | – |
| 1963-4 | 2 | 41 | 12 | 1 | – | 3 | – | 7 | 2 | – | – |
| 1964-5 | 2 | 27 | 15 | – | – | 1 | – | 5 | 4 | 2 | – |

\* Ivor is credited here with 12 goals, but one record shows him as having scored 13. The difference being that some records show an 'own goal'. We have included the lower figure here because, if ever there was any doubt as to who scored, Ivor always accepted the version which was not in his favour.

Ivor's final League game for the Bluebirds was against Rotherham on 24 April 1965 and resulted in a 3-2 win for Cardiff. The team on that occasion was: Wilson, Rodrigues, Baker, Williams, Murray, Hole, Johnston, Allchurch, Charles (J.), King, Lewis.

He scored two 'hat-tricks' for Cardiff, was leading scorer at the end of the 1963-4 season, and second top scorer for 1962-3. Ivor was club captain at Cardiff for season 1962-63.

We are grateful to Mark Adams of Porth for providing the data upon which this section is based.

★　　★　　★

## *At Newcastle United (1958-62)*

Ivor joined Newcastle in October 1958, he made his club and First Division début in a match against Leicester City at St. James's Park on 12 October 1958. Newcastle won 3-1 and Ivor scored twice. The team on that occasion was: Harvey; Keith, McMichael, Scoular, Stokoe, Bell, Hughes, Eastham, White, Allchurch, McGuigan.

### IVOR'S LEAGUE AND CUP APPEARANCES AND GOALS FOR NEWCASTLE

| Season | Div | League App | Gls | FA Cup App | Gls | FL Cup App | Gls | |
|--------|-----|------------|-----|------------|-----|------------|-----|--|
| 1958-9 | 1 | 26 | 16 | 1 | – | – | – | 2nd Top Scorer |
| 1959-60 | 1 | 41 | 13 | 2 | 1 | – | – | |
| 1960-1 | 1 | 36 | 7 | 4 | 3 | 1 | – | 2nd Top Scorer |
| 1961-2 | 2 | 40 | 10 | 1 | – | 2 | 1 | Top Scorer |

Ivor's final game for Newcastle was against Leeds United on 28 April 1962 at St. James's Park. Leeds won 3-0. The team on that occasion was: Hollins, Keith, Clish, Wright, Thompson, Turner, Day, Kerray, Thomas, Allchurch, Fell.

Ivor was club captain at Newcastle for periods during seasons 1960-1 and 1961-2.

_____

We are grateful to Paul Joannou, Official Club Historian and Archivist at St. James's Park, for providing the data upon which this section is based.

★  ★  ★

## At Swansea Town (1949-58)

Ivor joined the club as a professional in 1947.

His first team début was in a match against West Ham Utd. (away) on 26 December 1949. West Ham won 3-0. The team on that occasion was: Canning, Elwell, Keane, Paul, Weston, Burns, O'Driscoll, Lucas, Scrine, Allchurch, Beech (C.).

### IVOR'S LEAGUE & CUP APPEARANCES AND GOALS FOR THE SWANS

#### First Period

| Season | Div | League App | Gls | FA Cup App | Gls | Welsh Cup App | Gls | |
|--------|-----|--------|-----|--------|-----|--------|-----|---|
| 1949-50 | 2 | 18 | 3 | 2 | 1 | 2 | 1 | |
| 1950-1 | 2 | 42 | 8 | 1 | – | 1 | 1 | 2nd Top Scorer |
| 1951-2 | 2 | 41 | 11 | 3 | 3 | – | – | 2nd Top Scorer |
| 1952-3 | 2 | 41 | 15 | 1 | – | 1 | – | 2nd Top Scorer |
| 1953-4 | 2 | 40 | 17 | 3 | 2 | – | – | Top Scorer |
| 1954-5 | 2 | 36 | 20 | 4 | 1 | 3 | 2 | Top Scorer |
| 1955-6 | 2 | 37 | 13 | 1 | – | 3 | 3 | |
| 1956-7 | 2 | 30 | 11 | 1 | 1 | 4 | 1 | |
| 1957-8 | 2 | 32 | 14 | 1 | – | – | – | Top Scorer |
| 1958-9 | 2 | 10 | 6 | – | – | – | – | |

Ivor's final match of his first period at the Vetch was against Charlton Athletic at home on 27 September 1958. The game ended in a 2-2 draw, and Ivor scored. The team on that occasion was: King, Thomas

(D.), Lawson, Charles, Daniel, Brown, Allchurch (L.), Griffiths, Palmer, Allchurch (I), Morgan.

During the 1950-1 season he became the youngest Swansea Town player to have appeared in all 42 league matches during the season.

★　　★　　★

## *At Swansea Town (1965-68)*

Ivor's first match of his second period with the Swans' was away at Southend United on 21 August 1965. Southend won 2-0. The team on that occasion was: Black, Purcell, Hughes, Johnson, Jones, Williams (H.), Humphries, Draper, Todd, Allchurch, McLaughlin. Sub: Harley.

### IVOR'S LEAGUE & CUP APPEARANCES AND GOALS

Second Period

| Season | Div | League App | Gls | FA Cup App | Gls | FL Cup App | Gls | Welsh Cup App | Gls | Cup Win's Cup App | Gls |
|--------|-----|-----|-----|-----|-----|-----|-----|-----|-----|-----|-----|
| 1965-6 | 3 | 34 | 12 | 1 | – | 1 | 1 | 7 | 3 | – | – |
| 1966-7 | 3 | 44 | 13 | 3 | – | 4 | 2 | 1 | – | 2 | – |
| | | | | | | | | | | Top Scorer | |
| 1967-8 | 4 | 38/2 | 17 | 4 | 1 | 1 | 1 | 2 | 2 | – | – |
| | | | | | | | | | | Top Scorer | |

Ivor's final game for the club and his last in the Football League was against Hartlepools United at the Vetch on 6 May 1968. Hartlepools won 2-0. The team on that occasion was: Heyes, Evans (R.), Gomersall, Screen, Slee, Lawrence, Humphries, Williams (H.), Todd, Allchurch, Evans (B.). Sub: Thomas.

Ivor was club captain at the Vetch during seasons: 1953-4, 1955-6, 1956-7, 1966-7 (Part), 1967-8.

He was twenty when he made his league début and approaching his thirty-ninth birthday when he played his final game.

During the 1956-7 season, Ivor scored a goal in each of eight consecutive League matches; and during that period he scored a goal in each of nine consecutive League and Cup matches.

Whilst at the Vetch, Ivor scored six 'hat-tricks' and one 'four'.

Ivor was a member of the Swansea Town team which attracted the record gate to the Vetch Field. The match was against Arsenal on 17 February 1968 in the F.A. Cup, and there were 32,786 people in the ground. They saw Arsenal win by 1-0. Since this was Ivor's last F.A. Cup match, it is interesting to note that he played in his first and his last game in that competition against the London side. The games were separated by eighteen years.

He was involved in another record when playing at Leeds during the 1955-6 season. On 11 February 1956 three sets of brothers appeared in the same match. They were: Ivor and Len Allchurch, Cliff and Brin Jones, and John and Mel Charles. Big John was playing for Leeds.

★ ★ ★

# For Wales (1950-66)

Ivor made his début for Wales on 15 November 1950 versus England at Sunderland. England won 4-2. The team on that occasion was: Hughes, Barnes, Sherwood; Paul, Daniel, Lucas; Griffiths, Allen, Ford, Allchurch, Clarke.

## IVOR'S INTERNATIONAL APPEARANCES

| Versus | Date | Venue | Result | Scored | Club |
|---|---|---|---|---|---|
| England | 15.11.50 | Sunderland | 2-4 | | S |
| N. Ireland | 07.03.51 | Belfast | 2-1 | | S |
| Portugal | 12.05.51 | Cardiff | 2-1 | | S |
| Switzerland | 16.05.51 | Wrexham | 3-2 | | S |
| England | 20.10.51 | Cardiff | 1-1 | | S |
| Scotland | 20.11.51 | Glasgow | 1-0 | 1 | S |
| Rest UK | 05.12.51 | Cardiff | 3-2 | 2 | S |
| N. Ireland | 19.03.52 | Swansea | 3-0 | 1 | S |
| Scotland | 18.10.52 | Cardiff | 1-2 | | S |
| England | 12.11.52 | Wembley | 2-5 | | S |
| N. Ireland | 15.04.53 | Belfast | 3-2 | | S |
| France | 14.05.53 | Paris | 1-6 | 1 | S |
| Yugoslavia | 21.05.53 | Belgrade | 2-5 | | S |
| England | 10.10.53 | Cardiff | 1-4 | 1 | S |

| Versus | Date | Venue | Result | Scored | Club |
|--------|------|-------|--------|--------|------|
| Scotland | 04.11.53 | Glasgow | 3-3 | 1 | S |
| N. Ireland | 21.03.54 | Wrexham | 1-2 | | S |
| Austria | 09.05.54 | Vienna | 0-2 | | S |
| Yugoslavia | 22.09.54 | Cardiff | 1-3 | 1 | S |
| Scotland | 16.10.54 | Cardiff | 0-1 | | S |
| England | 10.11.54 | Wembley | 2-3 | | S |
| N. Ireland | 20.04.55 | Belfast | 3-2 | | S |
| England | 22.10.55 | Cardiff | 2-1 | | S |
| Scotland | 09.11.55 | Glasgow | 0-2 | | S |
| Austria | 23.11.55 | Wrexham | 1-2 | | S |
| N. Ireland | 11.04.56 | Cardiff | 1-1 | | S |
| Scotland | 22.10.56 | Cardiff | 2-2 | | S |
| England | 14.11.56 | Wembley | 1-3 | | S |
| Israel | 15.01.58 | Tel Aviv | 2-0 | 1 | S |
| Israel | 05.02.58 | Cardiff | 2-0 | 1 | S |
| N. Ireland | 16.04.58 | Cardiff | 1-1 | | S |
| Hungary | 08.06.58 | Sandviken | 1-1 | | S |
| Mexico | 11.06.58 | Stokholm | 1-1 | 1 | S |
| Sweden | 15.06.58 | Stokholm | 0-0 | | S |
| Hungary | 17.06.58 | Stokholm | 2-1 | 1 | S |
| Brazil | 19.06.58 | Gothenburg | 0-1 | | S |
| Scotland | 18.10.58 | Cardiff | 0-3 | | N |
| England | 26.11.58 | Villa Park | 2-2 | 1 | N |
| N. Ireland | 22.04.59 | Belfast | 1-4 | | N |
| England | 17.10.59 | Cardiff | 1-1 | | N |
| Scotland | 04.11.59 | Glasgow | 1-1 | | N |
| N. Ireland | 12.04.61 | Belfast | 5-1 | 1 | N |
| Spain | 19.04.61 | Cardiff | 1-2 | | N |
| Spain | 18.05.61 | Madrid | 1-1 | 1 | N |
| Hungary | 28.05.61 | Budapest | 2-3 | 1 | N |
| England | 14.10.61 | Cardiff | 1-1 | | N |
| Scotland | 08.11.61 | Glasgow | 0-2 | | N |
| Brazil | 12.05.62 | Rio | 1-3 | 1 | N |
| Brazil | 16.05.62 | Sao Paulo | 1-3 | | N |
| Mexico | 22.05.62 | Mexico City | 1-2 | | N |
| Scotland | 22.10.62 | Cardiff | 2-3 | 1 | C |
| Hungary | 07.11.62 | Budapest | 1-3 | | C |
| England | 22.11.62 | Wembley | 0-4 | | C |

| *Versus* | *Date* | *Venue* | *Result* | *Scored* | *Club* |
|----------|--------|---------|----------|----------|--------|
| Hungary | 20.03.63 | Cardiff | 1-1 | | C |
| N. Ireland | 03.04.63 | Belfast | 4-1 | | C |
| England | 12.10.63 | Cardiff | 0-4 | | C |
| Scotland | 03.10.64 | Cardiff | 3-2 | 1 | C |
| England | 18.11.64 | Wembley | 1-2 | | C |
| Greece | 17.03.65 | Cardiff | 4-1 | 2 | C |
| N. Ireland | 31.03.65 | Belfast | 5-0 | 1 | C |
| Italy | 01.05.65 | Florence | 1-4 | | C |
| USSR | 30.05.65 | Moscow | 1-2 | | S |
| England | 02.10.65 | Cardiff | 0-0 | | S |
| USSR | 27.10.65 | Cardiff | 2-1 | 1 | S |
| Scotland | 24.11.65 | Glasgow | 1-4 | 1 | S |
| Denmark | 01.12.65 | Wrexham | 4-2 | | S |
| | | | | | |
| Brazil | 14.05.66 | Rio | 1-3 | | S |
| Brazil 'B' | 18.05.66 | Bel Horiz'e | 0-1 | | S |
| Chile | 22.05.66 | Santiago | 0-2 | | S |

*Club code*:
S = Swansea Town; N = Newcastle United; C = Cardiff City.

Ivor's final cap was gained against Chile at Santiago, Chile won 2-0. The team on that occasion was: Millington; Rodrigues, Williams (G.), Hennessey, James (E. G.), Hole, Rees, Moore, Davies (R.), Allchurch, Pring. Subs: Davies (W.), Rankmore.

Ivor gained a total of 68 'caps', which remained a record for many years. He scored 24 international goals.

His international career encompassed sixteen years and he was approaching his 38th birthday when he played his final match against Chile.

# Index

*The Ivor we'll always remember.*